# THE RAILWAYMEN

# THE RAILWAYMEN

## R. S. JOBY

DAVID & CHARLES
Newton Abbot  London  North Pomfret (Vt)

**British Library Cataloguing in Publication Data**

Joby, R. S.
  The railwaymen.
  1. Railroads—Great Britain—Employees—History
  I. Title
  305.9'385'0941    HD8039.R12G8

  ISBN 0-7153-8010-9

Typeset by Typesetters (Birmingham) Ltd
and printed in Great Britain
by Redwood Burn Limited, Trowbridge, Wilts
for David & Charles (Publishers) Limited
Brunel House  Newton Abbot  Devon

Published in the United States of America
by David & Charles Inc
North Pomfret  Vermont 05053  USA

# Contents

TO MY FATHER
*who taught me to love railways*

# Introduction

A lifetime's work shapes a man in many ways, and his family too is moulded by his work patterns and moods. Railwaymen and their families have been involved in a love-hate relationship with the demands of the system for a century and a half. They provide a service to the public, for commuters, holiday-makers and business-people. For the family it means an alarm clock erupting at 4.30am on a cold foggy morning, a kettle whistling in the kitchen, a whiff of kippers, the toilet flushing, hobnailed boots marching down the street before dawn so that hundreds of season-ticket holders from the beech-woods of Buckinghamshire can get to their offices in good time. Night shifts ensure that the mail and newspapers arrive on breakfast tables. Weekends and holidays are still busy times for the railwayman and his family – they are in the public service and know its joys and sufferings.

From my earliest memories, just before World War II, railways have held centre stage. In those days father was a fireman at King's Cross Top Shed, a tall figure with blond hair, dressed almost always in blue overalls and grease cap. We lived in a large block of railway flats, cheek by jowl with Marylebone goods station. Engine whistles, hooters, the clink of buffers, the clop of the hooves of railway horses and activity in the coalyard and power station, were the dominant sounds of childhood. Railway life was a total and committed one. Many, such as the natural railwaymen, found the life satisfying; they were often third and fourth generation workers, a range of colourful characters, some bizarre, some congenial, who livened up messrooms and workbenches.

In the century and a half that railways have existed in this country, there have been several million railwaymen. They have included famous engineers, administrators like Geddes who made a national name for himself, and trade unionists like Jimmy Thomas and Ernie Bevin, who went on to become cabinet ministers, but the vast majority were the unsung men who quietly got on with an onerous job and did not give up, even under the most trying conditions. My father and uncle were amongst these men who did their best uncomplainingly as part of the team of hundreds of individual workers who together ensured that trains ran around the clock on any given main line. They and their modern counterparts have a story to tell which will be recognisable to all who have experienced or observed railway life.

To give a richer picture, I have gone into some detail about the background and domestic effects of railway life in relation to the railwayman I knew best, my father. The strains and stresses that shift work and rough job conditions put on the men and their families should not be glossed over, but neither should the compensations of railway life. The effort and teamwork that keeps the railways running well, despite problems with equipment and lack of capital investment, is backed up by families who only see their bread-winner in the evenings one week in three, where busy holiday periods are almost invariably marked by the absence of father, who is working so that others may be able to get to their resort. Service may be a derided word in some quarters these days, but that is what railwaymen give and have given for 150 years.

# 1

# The Building of a Disciplined Labour Force

When *Locomotion*, No 1, began regularly trundling along the Stockton & Darlington Railway in 1825, the first nucleus of railwaymen in the world came into being. Within a decade there were railways in several parts of the British Isles and by 1847 railwaymen numbered 50,000. This large work-force had been recruited and trained from a still mainly rural population which worked according to the dictates of night and day, got drunk regularly, contained large numbers of illiterates, and could be very unco-operative in matters of discipline. By trial and much error, by judicious application of both stick and carrot, the management of nearly a hundred different railways brought into being a group of men who worked by the clock, often nearly around the clock and whose skills were sought by other railways throughout the world.

There was no master-plan for creating the British railway system, nor was there one for training in new skills, either in railway work or in the factories sprouting in our major industrial areas. Learning by doing was the way with the pioneers, learning by 'sitting next to Nellie' was the way with their successors. The government interfered as little as possible, giving the directors of the railway companies maximum freedom to develop their systems. The directors in their turn wanted to be as free as possible to control their growing work-force. They were often magistrates or friends of magistrates, were opposed to unions, and working hard themselves, expected no less of their servants. An illustration of the problems of the first railways is afforded by the career of the original driver on the Great Western Railway.

The earliest specialised railwaymen were the drivers and firemen who obtained their initial training in the collieries of Tyneside and Lancashire, as well as on the early railways where Stephenson and Hackworth were the men who mattered. An example of one such driver was Jim Hurst, the first on the Great Western Railway. He was born at Astley, Lancashire, the son of cotton hand-loom weavers. He had no formal schooling and started work at the tender age of nine. He remembered having seen George Stephenson surveying Chat Moss in 1825, and when the family moved to Salford in 1830 for his father to take up a position as overseer of the Liverpool & Manchester Railway, he joined the railway as a labourer. The following year he mounted the footplate as a fireman and was promoted to driver in 1833.

The informal nature of recruitment was demonstrated by Jim Hurst being offered the Great Western job personally by Daniel Gooch. The locomotive engineer was working for the Vulcan Foundry near Warrington and had often ridden on Hurst's engine. He wanted him to work at Vulcan and then accompany the new broad gauge engines south by sea to London, thence by barge to West Drayton where they were put to work. The pay for the new engineman was 6/8d per day, or about £2 a week before deductions, a princely sum for the period for a young man of twenty-six.

Jim Hurst was in many ways a controversial character and may only have survived to retirement because of his connection with Daniel Gooch. He had left the Liverpool & Manchester Railway earlier than intended because his light engine collided with a train. Within three years of starting on the GWR he was 'fined 10/- for running his engine in a careless manner when pumping water on the main line and striking the *Wildfire* engine so as to break the frame and considerably injure his own tender on 4 September 1840'. This was a very light fine in the circumstances. Hurst must have been banished westwards to branch line work as we find a letter of complaint being sent to the GWR directors in 1842 as follows:

141 Powell, Policeman on the Branch has Reported to me that James Hurst is in the habit of taking people on the engine to and from Kemble and Cirencester, as many as three at a time. On the 28th of August he took two or three from Kemble but stopped the Engine about ¾ mile from Cirencester and put them Down. He also states that about two months since a couple of Farmers came on the Engine, one named Hart gave Herst [sic] money, he could not swear 6d or 1/-. But Herst thanked him, touched his cap and Pocketed the Money. Powell afterwards said "Mr Hart 1/- is a good deal of money for that distance. O said the latter I often ride".

On my questioning Tatlow Switchman at Kemble he says Hurst often takes people up and Down but he did not like to Report it.

Sir,
Yours Respectfully,
G. Rogers.

Driver Hurst was on a sacking charge for pocketing money that should have gone to the company. He was, however, able to produce the following letter, so the Houdini of the footplate lived to drive another day:

CIRENCESTER
*16 September 1842*

I hereby certify that Mr Jas. Hurst gave myself and brother a ride from Kemble in the morning of the 25th and 29th of August and that he neither *asked* nor did *receive* any money whatsoever for doing the same,

Signed,
Wm. W. Kershaw.

Such reporting of his activities by the railway police did not endear them to Jim Hurst. A year earlier he had been fined £2 for refusing to have a policeman on his train as a relief guard. In 1854 he accused a policeman of throwing a stone at his fireman near Bullo in the Forest of Dean. He wished to take the policeman into a field for a fight, but ended up with a 10/- fine. A couple of years later he was fighting a porter at Newnham, nearby, bringing a discharge upon himself, yet on appeal a mere six weeks later he was reinstated. The next six years brought him into increasing conflict with the authorities. In 1858 he ran past a danger signal at Farringdon Road, thus damaging a horse box. He damaged the tender of *Dart* at Reading in the following year and the buffers of *Alma* a few months later. Hurst's final removal from the footplate seems to have been in 1862 when he was sent from Maidenhead to Swindon as a fitter's labourer at the lower pay of 5/- per day. He finally retired in 1875, being given £100 as a lump sum, 12/- a week from the Enginemen & Firemen's Society, and a further 6/- a week from the Locomotive Sick Fund Society. This was further increased in 1888 by 6/- a week from GWR funds when it was realised that this historic old gentleman was still around. He died in 1892, outliving his patron Daniel Gooch by three years.

Although Britain had been industrialising for a century before the coming of the railways, there was no model on which their running could be based with confidence. The stagecoaches which they replaced had run regularly and kept good time in fine weather, but with their low capacity they gave few clues on how safety and high speed could be maintained in the new era. The established waggonways had a nucleus of platelayers who laid rails of cast and wrought iron on stone blocks. The operators of the waggonways employed men and boys to lead the horses, grease the waggons, make simple repairs and drive the alarmingly primitive steam engines.

But it required the genius of George and Robert Stephenson, Timothy Hackworth and their assistants to upgrade the scale and sophistication of railways to the point where they needed to employ large numbers of skilled and semi-skilled men over a wide area, working together under a stern discipline so that vast numbers of passengers and quantities of goods could be moved safely at speeds hitherto considered impossible. The Liverpool & Manchester Railway, on which Jim Hurst started his varied career, was the first railway in the world to bring all these skills together and prove that they could be made to work well and profitably.

The first decade of operation for the Liverpool & Manchester Railway established most of the features familiar in railway operation for more than a century afterwards, laid down the essential rules and regulations for safe operation, and also introduced the idea of a uniformed body of men loyal to the company. The methods used to attain these ends seem harsh to us: dismissal of drivers guilty of driving too fast and arriving early, imprisonment for the leaders of striking footplatemen, spells of duty lasting 16 and even 18 hours for week after week, dismissal for drunkenness and so on. Since a highly successful and very profitable railway was the end result, the practices of the Liverpool & Manchester were taken up by most of the early railways in Britain and overseas, while employees of that railway were eagerly sought, despite efforts by the directors to halt the drain of their employees by means of one-sided contracts. The employee could be dismissed on the spot, but if he wished to move elsewhere, he had to give up to three months' notice, a distinct disincentive to potential employers.

Safety and good timekeeping were the essentials of early railway discipline, drummed into employees by ever-growing rule books, wherein hundreds of rules governed their working lives in minute detail. There were even intrusions into private lives with enjoinders to church-going, not to mention personal appearance, drinking habits and honesty. The object was to bring into being a body of men with instinctive reactions of safety to train operating, willing to work where and when required, for as long as required, whose unquestioning loyalty could be taken for granted, but who could be sacked, fined or suspended for any infractions of the multitude of rules.

There was no shortage of men willing to submit to railway discipline in return for the relatively high and regular wages offered. Soldiers and sailors were an obvious source of recruits, accustomed to an even harsher discipline, which included flogging, but also able to dress smartly and take tough conditions in their stride, as well as being used to mobility. Farm labourers had the strength for portering jobs, and the more adaptable could be trained for the relatively simple signalling and guards' duties of the period. Mechanics from the mills were most useful in railway workshops, rapidly adapting their skills to the new medium. Stagecoach men found employment similar to their original calling, as guards and station staff. If recruits stood up well to the punishing hours and stringent routine of the new railways, promotion was available on the rapidly expanding railways of the 1840s and 1850s; for example, one could be running a small station within a few years of joining the railway as a junior clerk. The early engineers had even faster promotion thanks to their rarity. Daniel Gooch was not yet twenty-one when he was appointed to the Great Western Railway to take charge of their locomotives.

Those who stayed to make their careers with the railways started to form the steps in a graded structure which, in the course of time, became the accepted pattern for railway promotion. The grade system was based on the different categories of job offered by the railways and owed much to the military model. Locomotive men started as cleaners, then became passed cleaners who were allowed to fire locomotives before being promoted to firemen, who in turn became passed firemen, occasionally called on to drive. Drivers started with lowly jobs, shunting in the yard, short trip goods runs, finally with much luck and persistence reaching the top link in their fifties, unless they appeared to have the aptitude to become inspectors. Similarly porters and clerks became stationmasters, telegraph lads ended up as signal inspectors and so on across a range of hundreds of different jobs. The level of sophistication for higher posts increased throughout the nineteenth and twentieth centuries, but until recently, much of the learning process was, as in the earliest days, watching the practitioner and gradually obtaining the experience to do the job yourself. The multiplicity of grades had a result that suited Victorian managers very well. It was rare that different grades saw eye to eye on a common problem, thus making the divide and rule approach that much easier. It has made sectional strikes fairly easy to deal with and all-out strikes relatively rare.

The directors of our early railways could be ruthless with strikers, as the following example indicates:

*Yorkshire Gazette,* 22 September 1849

*Advertisement from the York, Newcastle & Berwick Railway.*

The directors of the York, Newcastle & Berwick Railway deeply regret that the Engine Drivers on their Main Line and Branches have entered into a Union against their employers, to Enforce an Unreasonable Demand for an Advance of Wages.

They beg to state that they have not given any Notice of a Reduction in Wages to any class of men. The men admit that they have no complaint whatever as to the manner in which they have been treated by the Locomotive Superintendent.

Wages of 4/- to 7/- per day are in line with those of other companies.

Arrangements are being made as will ensure the conducting of Passenger Traffic on their Line with perfect safety, by able and experienced Engine Drivers of good character.

*York, 21 September 1849.*

The able and experienced engine drivers frequently turned out to have been dismissed from other railways and were blacklegging in desperation.

Early railway operating practices were primitive, as were the responses of the hastily recruited staff on whom safety depended. Edward Bury, Engineer on the London & Birmingham Railway, was travelling on that line when he noted that a policeman guarding the entrance to Kilsby Tunnel was fast asleep. In a letter to Captain Moorsom he outlined the problems of running a railway with simple equipment and poorly trained manpower:

With regard to our Police I am certainly beginning to think it may be too numerous and inattention and neglect may be produced by having too large a number. Some alteration is requisite for they do not prevent accidents and it would be better for us to have none on the line and entirely depend on the Engine men only than have a body of men whose presence tends very much to decrease our vigilance. Probably we have not the right class of men, at all events they have to learn their duty and it can only be driven into their heads by actual experience. From letters this morning I learn an Engine was off the road at Birmingham Station yesterday by the Points being left open and at Wolverton two Engines had been in contact and one thrown off the Line.

*7 November 1838.*

No thought seems to have been given to the very long hours in all weathers that the men had to endure, but then the total commitment and endless hours that the engineers themselves spent trying to make their systems work may have induced a feeling that their servants should do likewise, although for much smaller rewards.

The London & Birmingham Railway expected its police to beat their stations for regular trains during the following hours:

Euston 7.00am–10.30pm
Tring 6.30am–8.30pm
Wolverton 5.30am–9.15pm
Birmingham 6.00am–10.30pm

They did, however, qualify for cottages at Wolverton for 1/6d per week, which may have been some compensation, had they been able to do more than merely sleep there.

The hardships and dangers of railway service were rewarded with above average pay in the early days. Even labourers on the Liverpool & Manchester Railway earned twice as much as they would have done on farms, while enginemen earning over £2 a week were the aristocrats of labour. High pay, high status and enormous pride in the job were hallmarks of a job on the railways. There was a feeling of being somebody different, a step above factory hands, farmworkers and the like. When the promotional ladder lengthened greatly in later Victorian times, ensuring that the better paid jobs only went to the middle-aged, it was still reckoned to be worthwhile doing mucky, ill-paid jobs for many years in order to reach the top. By that time family traditions had been established, providing an intake of the sons of railwaymen.

The years of grime and toil also served to winnow out those whose hearts were not totally committed to a railway career, incidentally providing the railways with cheap labour in the meantime. With such an endless supply, there was little incentive to mechanise: locomotives were hand fired throughout their service, goods were manhandled in most depots, cleaning of locomotives and stock was mostly manual until recently and the permanent way was kept in order by muscle power.

When traffic slackened, sacrifice from all was called for from the earliest times until the 1930s, as the example below indicates:

*Yorkshire Gazette, 3 November 1849*

MIDLAND RAILWAY

The board of directors are, it appears, actively engaged in carrying into effect the utmost economy and retrenchment of working expenses. Two of the more responsible officers at Derby have had their salaries reduced to the extent of £200 per annum., and yesterday week the 'pointsmen' along with the entire line received notice that their wages would be reduced to the extent of nearly 11%.

The 'pointsmen' who had hitherto worked 12 hours per day for 19/-per week, have met to consult upon this serious diminution of their wages, therefore they received with deepest regret a reduction to 17/-per week. They were employed 12 hours per day, 7 days a week and had no time allowed even for their meals. The saving over the whole line would be £400 a year, yet one collision on the line would destroy a larger amount of the company's property than they could save in 10 years.

Similar echoes and estimates have been heard in recent disputes.

Railwaymen were different, whether they lived in the railway tenements in Glasgow, the Great Western garden villages or the Great Central settlements at Marylebone and Neasden, to name but a few. These settlements told of a community apart from the weekday workers on permanent day work. Railwaymen not only worked shifts, including Sundays and holidays, but long hours of overtime were also expected when there was a rush or a crisis, so they tended to mix with each other, have social clubs with flexible hours suited to their work, and to be much more ready to relocate themselves should the railway company desire. There was solidarity reinforced by trades unions, despite grading divisions, and a recognisable common purpose.

One of the benefits of a railway career was early recognition of holidays. The railways pioneered an annual holiday for employees in the 1890s, insisted on benefit society membership, an early form of health insurance, while giving support to savings schemes, sports and cultural clubs, station gardening and a host of other beneficial activities. Housing in railway towns and elsewhere was also important. Privilege tickets enabled employees to travel in their limited spare time, later extended to their offspring travelling independently, which was the greatest boon of a railway childhood.

Pride in the job sums up the attitude of the traditional railwayman. Few careers in this century have kept their employees for such lengthy portions of their lives and still fewer have left such an indelible impression on them. It is difficult to imagine soap packers reminiscing about soap they have packed, fishmongers about fish they have filletted, but start a railwayman recalling his career and you will be there until the early hours. Moreover, they communicate their enthusiasm to those who were never in railway employment. It is the mystique of most aspects of railway work that makes thousands flock each weekend to preserved railways to scrape paint off rusty boilers, remove ash from pits, shovel coal on a bucking footplate for no return other than the satisfaction of working on the railway. Holidays spent as guards, cleaners or platelayers appeal to clergymen, stockbrokers and salesmen as well as working railwaymen.

The deep satisfaction expressed by railwaymen in a range of occupations contrasts strongly with the boredom and listlessness so common in many other jobs. The work and discipline formula worked out by George Stephenson and the Liverpool & Manchester Railway directors a century and a half ago has had to be modified with changing social conditions, but the core of safety and teamwork persists to make rail travel still the safest and most pleasant means of transport invented by man.

# 2
# Station and Office Work

On the manual side of railway work, the position of driver was seen as the most glamorous, but office and station work was often more rewarding and a good deal less strenuous. Indeed the promotion ladder could lead to management positions for the very able and fortunate. Entry depended on literacy, but having a father already on the railway helped a great deal, as the case of Joseph Tatlow shows in mid-Victorian times:

> In the year 1867, at the age of sixteen, I became a junior clerk in the Midland Railway at Derby, at a salary of £15 a year . . .
> From pre-natal days I was destined for railway service, as an oyster to its shell. The possibility of any other vocation for his sons never entered the mind of my father, nor the mind of many another father in the town of Derby.

Those not from railway families did not have Tatlow's head start in the keen competition to secure a position on the railway. No less a personality than Karl Marx attempted to secure a clerical post with the Great Western Railway at the same period but was rejected because of poor handwriting. Had the railway taken him on, he would never have completed *Das Kapital.* Requests for such posts came from all over the British Isles, as this letter from a young Irish hopeful shows:

> Castletown,
> Portroe,
> *4 May 1908*

Dear Sir,
    As I have finished my schooling, I take the advantage of asking you to appoint me to your service. I am a Tipperary man and perhaps you

have a liking for those on account of the late Mr J. Hogan who was so well liked by all the Railway servants. I live near his native town and will send you testimonials from his friends, the High Sheriff of the County and other well known gentlemen if you say you will take me on. I am 18 years and need scarcely say that I am a total abstainer. I can show my certificates for passing final and mid grades in the following subjects, Arithmetic, Algebra, Book-keeping, French, Shorthand, English Literature and Composition and Science. I will be pleased to abide by any rules you make for me. Hope you will not disappoint me.

Yours etc.
Daniel Sullivan.

The letter was marked 'no chance' and then filed under 'Odd and humorous correspondence' in the GWR files, presumably because of the personal tone.

Those fortunate enough to be considered were interviewed and examined as well if the jobs required numeracy and literacy on any scale. Early days on the job were frequently difficult unless one had a sympathetic mentor, lacking in the case of Joseph Tatlow, to whom we return:

My railway life began on a drizzling dismal day in the early autumn. My father took me to the office in which I was to make a start and presented me to the chief clerk. I was a tall, thin, delicate, shy, sensitive youth, with dark curly hair, worn rather long, and I am sure I did not look at all a promising specimen for encountering the rough and tumble of railway work.

The chief clerk handed me over to one of his assistants, who without ceremony seated me on a high stool at a high desk, and put before me, to my great dismay, a huge pile of formidable documents which he called Way Bills. He gave me some instructions, but I was too confused to understand them, and too shy to ask questions. I only knew that I felt very miserable and hopelessly at sea. Visions of being dismissed as an incompetent rose before me; but soon, to my great relief, it was discovered that the Way Bills were too much for me and that I must begin on more elementary duties.

Many other careers started with such problems, but Tatlow later became general manager of the Midland Great Western Railway.

Station staff were the most visible of the railway's representatives and the stationmaster was the main contact with the upper classes and merchants who provided most of the income for the early railways. A considerable effort was therefore made to acquire trustworthy and presentable men for this publicly important work. Branwell Brontë, son of a vicar and brother of Charlotte, was commended to the Manchester & Leeds Railway but did not last long due to his fondness for the bottle. The most detailed account of recruitment for station posts in mid-Victorian times is given by Ernest Simmons who was taken on by the GWR early in 1861. He was the son of a failed farmer, who nevertheless had good connections with the vicar of his old parish and a second cousin who was a lawyer in London. This cousin provided an introductory letter to a director of the GWR who

> was reading my cousin's letter of introduction and appeared to be somewhat amused by its contents. He addressed me in French, and having satisfied himself that I was tolerably proficient in that language, he enquired in English if I really could carry a sack of beans . . .
>
> I was directed to wait outside for Mr Badger. He soon joined me, and after I had accompanied him to a very snug office and signed a form of application in which there was a clause which provided that nothing should be claimed in case I was killed, he informed me that the next day was Board day for the appointment of clerks, and that as Mr Butcher had told him that I was anxious to get on the railway at once, I should lose no time in getting the necessary testimonials, amongst which should be one from a clergyman who had known me.

The interview itself was something of an anti-climax. The directors examined the testimonials, and Simmons was then asked if he would like 'to go on at once' after being asked a few perfunctory questions, with no hint of duties or salary. He was sent to Oxford the following day and received an initial salary of £60 per annum, rising to stationmaster status just over two years later at the age of twenty-three.

Conditions in offices and stations varied enormously. The Paddington accounts office in 1861 was like an immense schoolroom, only that the boys had whiskers and most of them were out at the elbows, and all looked miserably thin; moreover, they were all standing to write, and the bundles of papers before each were enough to turn each poor fellow's heart sick. At the head of the table sat a deformed gentleman of about fifty years of age; he had worked his way up from being an ordinary clerk, and had joined the railway from its commencement. He always came to business at 8.45am and never left until 6pm, and invariably subsisted on a biscuit and a glass of water during the day . . . Many of the poorest of the clerks of necessity followed his example and when the clock struck One they quietly pulled out their drawer and ate a piece of dry bread and cheese.

Matters were much less formal at stations away from head office, where there was a variety of staff and the stationmaster and his clerks were the élite. Ernest Simmons certainly felt himself to be part of an élite when he wrote that

a stationmaster at a small station was then [1863] a personage of greater importance in the estimation of the public than he is now [1879]. It was a new thing, and the clerks and stationmasters were for the most part supplied from the middle class of society, and able to hold their own in a gentlemanly way; whereas at the present day, they are for the most part, descendants of the porters, and policemen, who, having been educated in the British and Free schools, have been drafted into the Telegraph Office, and thence into clerks' appointments. There is nothing sharpens the wit like a telegraph office, but it cannot be expected that the associations of their homes will make them conversant with the habits and manners of gentlemen.

The expansion of railway staff and the increased openings for young gentlemen in other callings were also responsible for the changes noted. The working-class lads thus promoted were also willing to accept lower pay and the harsher conditions of stations like Weston. Weston was a small station in the Fens near Spalding. Unlike stations to the east of King's Lynn, it had been built in the 1860s, and by 1895 was clearly inadequate for staff accommodation. A letter from the Surgeon of the Great Northern & Midland Joint Railway at Spalding shows how desperate the situation had become:

*9 March 1895*
Spalding

Before Mr Ostler, the present Clerk in Charge, took up his residence here there was [sic] two cases of Diptheria – one of which proved fatal to a daughter of the then Clerk in Charge Mr Morley.

These cases at the time were attributed by us to the insanitary condition of the house. I believe a report was made at the time. I need go very little into detail. An inspection of the premises I am sure is all that is necessary to answer having things put right, but I may say the horrible stench prevading [sic] the whole of the ground floor rooms and particularly the office was so overpowering that I had to make a hurried exit to obtain something like fresh air.

The well water is undoubtedly contaminated from the pit across the line and the closet arrangements leave a great deal to be desired.

Wm. L. Byham of Barritt & Byham, Surgeons.

It further emerged in subsequent correspondence that the pantry was formerly an old water closet and that the cesspit was immediately under the structure. But help was at hand. William Marriott, the newly appointed engineer of the line wrote to Derby less than a fortnight later, strongly recommending action:

Telegrams-Marriott, Railway,
Melton Constable
*20 March 1895*

The present Station accommodation is one room 10½ feet by 10 feet out of which comes the Booking Office. The house accommodation is one kitchen 9½ feet by 8½ feet, a sleeper shed used as a living room 10 feet square and two bedrooms. The Station Master, his Wife and eight children live in this house. The water supply is bad being evidently contaminated by three Cesspools.

After these letters, a new and well-appointed house costing £360 was sanctioned, although 'all unnecessary expense is to be avoided'.

The rural stationmaster in pre-nationalisation days was one of the village or small town élite. Together with the vicar, publican, policeman and the better-off farmers, he received a relatively

23

good income, but with the privileges and status came many onerous duties.

There were well over a hundred village and small market town stations strung out across north Norfolk before the closures of the 1950s and later. They had been built either by the former Great Eastern Railway or by the Midland & Great Northern Joint Railway and its predecessors. Some towns and villages like Cromer, Fakenham and Aylsham even had two stations thanks to past competitive building, while Cromer could boast a halt as well on the only joint railway in the country owned by another joint railway, the Norfolk & Suffolk Joint Railways, which was owned by the M&GNJR and the GER. Such were the local complexities of ownership, but whatever the situation, the stationmaster was the man on the spot, responsible to head office in London or King's Lynn for the thousand and one aspects of running his station efficiently and watching over the lines either side of the station. He usually had a house in or near the station. The stationmaster's house at Mundesley was part of a terrace of eleven, built 'in a superior manner', rather better than the rest of the terrace, designed for humbler grades of railwaymen.

The stationmaster had status and had to be seen to have it in a number of ways. His uniform was better cut and had gold braid, his cap was larger, his gold watch in its fob pocket worn from the innumerable times that it had been pulled out for consultation. Depending on the importance and traffic, the man in charge had to oversee any number of subordinates from one to fifty and was ultimately responsible for the smooth running of his little section of the system.

A M&GN stationmaster before World War I earned between 30/- and 37/6d per week, nearly twice as much as his non-clerical staff. For this he was on nearly continuous call, as trains came through for up to twenty hours continuously, even on Sundays in summer when there was a great deal of excursion traffic. However, by judicious delegation, he certainly would not work for twenty hours. A fleet-footed lad porter, endowed with a sixth sense of where to find the stationmaster when needed, helped a great deal in the days before telephones were found in country stations. Messages could be taken for passing on, thus guaranteeing the stationmaster a good night's sleep, the eating of his meals in relative peace and the ability to have a quiet pint in a nearby hostelry, naturally while on business. No higher authority could arrive other than by rail and subordinates could be primed as to how to reply should the telegraph demand an instant answer. In the early years of the twentieth century, a stationmaster even qualified for a fortnight's holiday a year, rare indeed amongst working men at the time.

Larger stations had an elaborate hierarchy of employees, with the stationmaster at the apex of a pyramid of sometimes arbitrary power. Titles differed as between companies, but the uniformed staff were usually controlled in day-to-day matters by a station foreman, sometimes known as a working foreman. He was also in charge in the absence of the stationmaster. The clerical staff, manning booking, parcels, and goods offices, were answerable to the stationmaster but were graded separately and were also salaried, even when they took home mere shillings per week, thus distinguishing them radically from the uniformed staff. This also applied to their dress and sometimes to their pretensions.

The stationmaster's staff ranged from lad porters to booking and goods clerks, station foremen in larger stations, as well as shunters, signalmen, telegraph messengers, goods porters and draymen, while the platelayers and crossing-gate keepers kept in contact with headquarters through the station. Every day, the stationmaster received a leather pouch from headquarters at King's Lynn containing instructions, forms, notices, invoices, requests, all demanding instant action. Even more urgent messages came in over the single needle telegraph, whose morse clicking spelt out delays, cattle trucks gone astray and a host of other daily crises along the line. Through it, messages official and unofficial passed along a hundred miles of railway, open to all who could crack the code. All that the inquisitive passenger

25

heard and saw was a whirring and clacking of a needle possessed, should he poke his nose into the inner sanctum.

Once trained, most of the staff knew their jobs without further orders and could cope in most emergencies. The rule book, always in theory and generally in practice, had an answer to any problems encountered in day-to-day working, but the stationmaster was the final local arbiter in case of ambiguities. If he were puzzled, a telegraph message to headquarters might produce a solution, for there worked the experts.

The lad porter learned by having the simple and usually tedious or unpleasant jobs explained and delegated to him. The lamp room was very important in days of oil lighting. Trimming wicks, filling the vessel with oil, testing and relighting, checking the paraffin canister and reordering, were all vital but messy jobs. In the booking office tickets were checked against the accounts before the date stamp was altered to start another day. New batches of tickets had to be ordered well ahead of likely use in order to allow for printing delays. A good booking clerk knew traffic patterns well enough never to run short. There were other tickets that had been supplied when the station opened and could be guaranteed to last until the end of the century. Meanwhile in the goods office, parcels were sorted according to the trains they were to be loaded on, up or down side, express or local. The stationmaster could quickly compare labels and ledgers to make sure that everything had been entered and charged up properly from the thousands of scales in the fat books of parcels and goods rates. What did one charge a stage magician moving his props from Cromer to Sheffield at the end of the summer season? It was all there, somewhere.

Arrivals and departures were the high points of the day. Long experience told the stationmaster where the guard's van of each train would stop, so that the parcels and post trolleys could be stationed on the edge of the platform, nicely adjusted to allow the guard to fling open the door at the right spot. Two porters were usually used to pass and stack the outgoing items in the van, then rapidly to evacuate those destined for the station under the eagle eye of the passenger guard. No surreptitious removal of a strawberry chip or a wing of skate would occur if he could help it. Complaints about missing parcels soon caught up with the staff responsible, whose record would be marred with a reprimand for slackness or worse. The village postman would exchange his mailbags with the guard, and within half a minute of arrival, the green flag could be waved after a quick visual check to see that doors were closed, affirmed by a nod from the station foreman. Stopping trains in the early years of the century were no mere nuisances cluttering up the line and preventing expresses from keeping time; they were a vital constituent of service to town and village alike and well patronised. A prime cheese for the manor, a case of tea for the grocer, a letter from a son in Australia, they all came by train, usually promptly and in good condition.

The station forecourt was active for much of the day. Pony and trap kept farm, village, town and station in touch with each other. Bicycles were important, too, for delivery and for bringing passengers to the station where they were stored in the left luggage room while the owner went off to town. Collection and delivery, messages to shopkeepers, requests for cattle wagons and horseboxes went to and fro by messenger. The stationmaster emerged periodically from his office to pass the time of day and exchange farming news with his customers, before taking a stroll around the station yard, then back along the platforms, making sure that everyone was doing his appointed task. By 10.00am the gents' toilet should be polished, swilled out and reeking of Jeyes Fluid. The porters should be weeding the rosebeds by 10.15am in the lull between trains, as the annual station garden competition was approaching and a first-class certificate would be an asset in any booking hall, a worthy trophy that passengers could see. Dirty footprints and streaks from recent rain on the white edging to the platform indicated that another coat of whitewash was overdue, while some floor polish on the lino in the ladies waiting room would not come amiss. When the water level in the station tank was low, usually after a dry spell, the lad porter would be detailed to pump underground supplies up by handpump, a task that would keep him out of mischief for several hours.

Many of these concerns were doubtless petty, as the nation found out in wartime when, despite staff reductions, trains still ran efficiently even if stations did look a mess, but the men who made the stations look a picture took a real pride in the job; to them slackness was a sin. A high standard of appearance once attained was easy to keep up if the whole team co-operated, but difficult to return to if pride diminished.

The goods yard was a special concern of the stationmaster. Wagons were scarce, delay was expensive and if demurrage bills arrived, it was the boss who was on the carpet, even if he had delayed loading to oblige an important farmer or merchant customer. A constant battle of wits was waged between the traffic department and stationmasters, and between them and the customers. Seasonal peaks and gluts produced wagon shortages, so that bags of potatoes or cabbages could be seen in cattle wagons, hopefully hosed clean. The customer would try to get as many wagons as he could, the traffic department would stint a stationmaster who had had empty wagons in his sidings, so the man in the middle knew what it felt like to be a grain of wheat in a flour mill. Nevertheless, the old hands had influence and could often conjure up wagons where none was reported to exist. New men either got wise to the tricks of the trade quickly or their promotion came to an abrupt halt.

Coal merchants received loaded wagons from the colliery companies and then tended to use them for storage, thus cluttering up the sidings and annoying the colliery as well, for the colliery did not dare remonstrate too hard for fear of losing a customer. Ten tons of coal was no great amount for an industrial user, but for a country coal merchant it was a week's supply and he objected to having to empty the wagon and then fill up the sacks from his coal wharf. It was much easier to fill the sacks from the wagon so the coal siding tended to go on being cluttered and was useless for general goods wagons.

Staff could deputise for each other in the same type of work and this was one of the main ways in which juniors learned their jobs. A porter could cover for his foreman, an experienced telegraph messenger for his signalman under supervision, the clerks could do the stationmaster's paperwork for a few days, knowing that if their authority was flouted, the recalcitrant would receive his come-uppance when the boss returned. Each man was a vital link in running the station and the line, but teamwork of a high order meant that no one was irreplaceable.

Larger stations had a company dray and horse, which might also be used for shunting. In East Anglia before 1914, locomotives cost about 6/- per hour while shunting, so a horse that cost less than £1 a week was an obvious saving in a small station, or one with less goods traffic. The drayman was paid 1/- to come in to feed and water the horse on Sunday, after working a full six day week going the rounds of collecting and delivering, dressed in a massive leather apron, corduroys and gaiters.

Station staff coped with emergencies very well on the whole, never allowing fixed ideas of duty hours to interfere with their sense of responsibility to the travelling public. The great flood of 31 August 1912 inundated the M&GN line at Aylsham, so that a row of cottages near the station was submerged to the level of the bedrooms. A train in the station at the time of the flood could move neither forward nor backward, so the two hundred-odd passengers were bedded down as best as possible in the train and station rooms. Staff waded into town, which was above the floodwaters, to fetch milk for the babies and children and to obtain provisions for the adult passengers. Some of the men worked non-stop for thirty-six hours, and after the floodwaters receded, put in many hours of overtime on an already long day to clear up the mess and get traffic running normally again.

The co-ordination of the work of stations and other sections of the railway service was done in divisional or national head offices from where inspectors and auditors descended at irregular intervals on station, depot and works. All books had to be in order, copied in a fair hand. In the early days such visits often resulted in sackings because of incompetence or deficiencies of one sort or another from the inexperienced clerical staff, but gradually a body of method was built up and the men who operated the system adjusted well to it. Rules, traditions and customs in tackling the mass of paperwork generated by far-flung systems were not greatly changed between Victorian times and the computer age. Card tickets, way bills, hand-written invoices and ledgers were still part of the scene when Dr Beeching reported, a century after Ernest Simmons mastered his first station.

As in the days of which Simmons wrote, the mid-twentieth-century stationmaster led a peripatetic life if he wished to be promoted. Geoffrey Chappell started his career in the time-honoured way as an assistant in Bury St Edmunds goods office, and by 1946 was in charge of a staff of five at Harling Road station on the Norwich to Ely line. Life at his next appointment in the 1950s, the junction station of Wroxham, was very different, with pick-up goods trains especially busy in the sugar beet season, while during the summer thousands of boat hirers for the Broads passed through the station. So busy was it that it supported a bookstall until 1965. His final move was to North Walsham where goods traffic dominated. Both the former GER and M&GN yards were in full use in 1960, serving much of north Norfolk with its granary, coalyard, parcels and general goods service. A large canning factory next to the station filled several wagons daily in season, while farm produce and stores kept a staff of fourteen very active. Yet change came so fast that by the late 1960s most of this traffic had gone, the passenger side was an unstaffed halt and the stationmaster retired. (One is driven to ask, after seeing similar lines thriving in Europe, need it have been thus?)

# 3

# *The Way They Used to Live*

Railwaymen worked the hours set by the company. Through most of railway history the higher grades at least earned above average wages, but being at the beck and call of the company, had to live within a short distance of their often isolated workplace. These factors meant that railwaymen often lived in groups, and where no other accommodation was available, it was provided by the company. These properties ranged from the clay-lump cottages for crossing keepers built by the Thetford & Watton Railway for £150 each, to substantial dwellings for shedmasters in isolated locations. At its peak in the years before World War I, railway accommodation must have housed in excess of a quarter of a million men, women and children, plus their inevitable lodgers. Due to the exigencies of such service, the way railway families used to live developed its own momentum and customs, geared to shifts or the hooter in the workshop towns.

In addition to the conditions which are described in the chapter on works towns, there were a huge number of other railway settlements around the country, ranging from a clutch of cottages miles from anywhere at such spots as Riccarton Junction in the remote border region, or Roudham Junction in Norfolk's Breckland, which had no road access or services other than those supplied by the railway. At a quite different level, minor towns and villages like March, Woodford Halse, Severn Tunnel Junction, or Carnforth were converted into major traffic centres by the railway, whose goods yards, engine shed and station provided hundreds of new jobs where only a few farm-hands had been needed before. In such circumstances the railway community swamped the other local community so that services and life generally were geared to its needs. The railway company frequently endowed a school, hospital and a place of worship, as well as making contributions or land available for leisure pursuits. In return it expected absolute co-operation from the work-force.

The crossing-keeper's gatehouse was usually the humblest type of railway accommodation. In the rolling acres of East Anglia and the Fens they were almost as abundant as the poppies that decorated the cornfields, well over a hundred of them in Norfolk alone! The M&GN line had about one every two miles, inhabited usually by a platelayer and his wife or a retired or disabled employee glad of a roof over his head, a garden for his vegetables and a few shillings of pension. The day was a long one, starting at 6.30am and continuing until the last train just before 9.00pm. When weekend excursions were running in the summer the job went right around the clock. Where the gate was close to a signal box, early warning of a train was easily obtained by listening to the bells or watching the signals. Elsewhere the timetable and a careful lookout were needed to avoid the ultimate indignity of 'losing your gates'. An unread special notice or unusually early running of the first train had to be taken into account. Where the wife opened and shut the gates, the dual income from platelayer or signalman husband gave the couple a standard of living well above that of other local workers. The cottages were small but snug and usually a fire would be kept going the whole time, summer and winter as the keeper had to venture out in all weathers. The gate lamps needed filling with oil, their wicks trimmed and their bull's eye lens polished, all done between calls at roughly hourly intervals for gate opening and closing. The life was isolated but very popular until the 1950s when demands for higher rates and overtime made level crossings on secondary lines so costly that they were closed down or automated as quickly as possible.

In extreme contrast to the rural isolation of the level crossing was a block of flats owned by the Great Central Railway

A lad porter at Whaplode between Spalding and King's Lynn on the Midland & Great Northern Joint Railway. Note the characteristic somersault signal which has its spectacle and lamp, seen in the boy's hand, lower down the post (*Lens of Sutton*)

The stationmaster and his daughters at Llanishen on the Rhymney Railway line between Caerphilly and Cardiff, taken in 1908. Stationmasters generally lived 'on the job', in a part of the station building if it was substantial, or in a specially provided dwelling adjacent to the station (*Lens of Sutton*)

The booking office at Leicester Central, Great Central Railway, in 1898. Notice the racks of Edmondson card tickets (*S.W.A. Newton Collection, Leicester Library & Record Office*)

constructed in 1895 to house their work-force and some of the people displaced by the demolition of 37 acres of houses for the new Marylebone terminal. About 1,500 people were crammed on to just over 4 acres of land squeezed between the Regent's Canal and St John's Wood Road. It was an odd situation for working-class flats, with Lord's cricket ground and the homes of the very rich surrounding it, but the nearest other available land was at Neasden near Cricklewood, where the railway built its engine sheds and established another colony of railwaymen. The flats were sycophantically named Wharncliffe Gardens after the company's chairman. A host of people from Sheffield, Nottingham, Manchester and others locally recruited were brought together here and at other points along the line. Over a two year period the staff numbers built up as first a goods service and then passenger and parcels services started.

Most of the flats had but two rooms with kitchen and toilet, although there were about a hundred with three rooms, and fifty with four rooms. In the latter, for architectural reasons, the toilet was built within the kitchen. The coal bunker was under the draining board, making for very messy coal deliveries, while of course no bathrooms were provided, despite the mucky occupations of most of the tenants. At least there was cold running water and a flush toilet, and in the living room a range that heated water for the engineman's scrub in the tub before the fire, cooked the food and heated at least one room. As late as the 1950s rents were between 10/- and £1 a week. Narrow courtyards separated the blocks, zealously swept by the yardmen, who also took it upon themselves to stop most games on the grounds that they either involved balls or were too noisy. Fortunately Regent's Park was within walking distance.

An early resident of the 'Gardens', Ron Andrew, has penned some lines which other older residents assure me give the authentic feel of the railway colony in the early years of the century:

I lived in Wharncliffe Gardens in the happy days of yore;
My childhood days were spent there, as were those of many more.
Old Wharncliffe was a village, before the First World War –
And hordes of happy children found the courtyards not a bore.

The days of youth they quickly passed, though much there was to tell;
The hours were marked at mealtimes by the clanking Stoneyard bell.
In World War One air raids began, the policemen cried "Take cover",
The Zeppelins came over, and new times we did discover.

Emmanuel Church just round the corner used our Wharncliffe boys,
To fill its choir – they truly did – and made a cheerful noise.
On Treat Days at Emmanuel, Mr Bates's CLB
(The Boys' Brigade) marched three sides round old Wharncliffe to our
glee.

In front of church Rev J.V.M. took General Salute,
And bugle-blowing Boys' Brigade marched off – we followed suit.
The station at St John's Wood Road was reached ('twas quite a
scramble),
And Sunday School got into train for Ruislip and a ramble.

The smelly landings that we had before gas lamps were lit;
And I recall some families were forced to moonlight flit.
But many Wharncliffe families had window box displays,
Sweet peas and other flowers nicely perfumed summer days.

We played cricket at the lamp post, by Grove Road Catholic Church,
And scrumped the iron-hard pears near there, on branches we would
perch.
We saw the homing horses clopping Lisson Grove along,
To reach the railway stables in Lodge Road there to throng.

The coalyard where we queued, the rationed coal to get;
I queued there with my mother – a thing I shan't forget.
And later Wharncliffe's coal was stored in piles around the backs;
And children played at hide and seek among the grimy stacks.


The Great Central Railway dominated most aspects of life in
the area. The stables in Lodge Road serviced the huge goods
depot fronting on Lisson Grove. The double-storey stables were
in partial use until 1950, ruled by a fiery Irishman, Mr Platt,
who lived in a railway cottage opposite. In his heavy boots, long
leather apron and a red face bisected by a huge walrus

moustache, he imposed order and discipline on both horses and carters. The cobbled yards rang with the huge iron-shod hooves of the cart-horses. It was always a favoured stopping point going to and from the park, followed by a look over the approaches to Lord's Tunnel, where A5 tanks or A3 Pacifics on expresses would burst out in a pall of sulphurous smoke, so different in taste and smell from Paddington.

Like most large families that had settled in a railway community, the Joby family gradually colonised several of the flats in Wharncliffe Gardens as sons and daughters married and produced their own families. Charlie was a driver on the Metropolitan, a veteran of the Inner Circle in steam days when he fired in an open cab. Bobby fired at King's Cross, while Stan, my father, started at Neasden just before the grouping, later transferring to King's Cross and then to Stratford for a decade before returning to Neasden as a driver in 1948. Other relatives lived at Neasden and Swindon in railway colonies, a cousin married into a Midland family from Cricklewood, while my sister crowned the process by marrying the grandson of Thomas Worsdell of the North Eastern Railway. In such an atmosphere one lived, breathed and totally absorbed a railway atmosphere.

Other neighbours were from many grades in the railway service. Next door lived a porter who worked on the Metropolitan Railway, very conscious of having been in charge of Marlborough Road station before it closed. Out of uniform he always wore a bowler hat and raincoat regardless of the weather and identified with clerical tenants rather than other manual grades. The clerks were also acutely aware of their status. Neat but threadbare suits, immaculate shirts, briefcases and trilby hats were their accoutrements as they set off for the office after 8 o'clock each morning. Their wives were equally well aware of their higher status in life, while their children had names like Roger, Keith and Elizabeth rather than the Dave, Stan and Gloria of commoner folk. They tended to organise courtyard parties, collect for worthy causes and be the officials in the local churches, where their regular hours must have been a great help.

Train crews were a significant minority, whose irregular hours must have been a trial to their families and their neighbours. Typically a family of four or five had only three rooms and a scullery to live in. It took seventeen years of waiting before our family moved to a larger flat, while one family of nine lived in a three-roomed flat until the older children moved out. The stone steps and the concreted narrow courtyards rang to the sound of hobnailed boots at almost any hour of day and night as the overalled men went to and fro. On the top floor of our block lived a King's Cross fireman with his wife and young child. A regular Friday night job that he had in summer was to bring the carriages of the Fort William sleeping car train into platform 10 at King's Cross, take things easy for the next three hours, then take the N2 tank engine back to the locomotive shed and walk the two miles across Camden Town to his home. On one fateful night he had lost his key, a fact which he did not seem to discover until he had clumped up ten flights of stairs and woken many of the neighbours. The knockers on the doors were huge cast-iron Victorian monsters; the doors themselves massive thick hardwood joinery of real railway quality. An almighty bang failed to wake the wife at about 2.00am; she was known to be a heavy sleeper, but any neighbours not awake before certainly were by now. The sound of door knocker, hobnailed boot and louder and louder cries of, 'Lill, open the . . . door!' went on for a good half hour before having the required result. Later it was arranged to leave a spare key with a less slumbrous neighbour to prevent repetition.

The closeness of everybody to each other meant that family rows, wife beating, even family secrets became widely known almost instantly. Male social life revolved around two pubs, one of which was managed by an uncle. Few of the wives ever went there as they were discouraged by social pressures and the need to clean and cook constantly in an area where a power station and railway yards poured a constant rain of smoke, dust and smuts on their handiwork. A set of curtains would turn the water black three times before proper washing could be started. Greasy overalls were left to soak for two days in a soda solution before a final wash and rinse. Yet despite the problems, most of the flats were spotlessly clean, as were the landings and courtyards. Those who let things slip would soon know about it from their neighbours.

The village type of community had its advantages in bad times. Latch-key kids hardly existed even in war time, while families who were slack in this respect faced severe censure. Mothers ruled the roost domestically while fathers earned the wages. Older daughters were expected to help out as soon as they were old enough, escorting younger ones to school or the shops. Less was expected of the boys at home, but newspaper rounds, milk rounds and other ways of helping the family budget were their prerogative.

To take the specific example of my own family, mother and father moved into their own flat in 1932, having tried unsuccessfully living with his parents until they had saved enough for a house deposit. As a fireman at King's Cross my father earned about £3 a week and my mother a little less as a tailoress working in Savile Row. Rent at 10/- (50p) a week meant that they had little incentive to take on the higher cost and greater responsibility of a mortgage, so they stayed in Wharncliffe Gardens surrounded by his family. Many established young railwaymen moved out at that time to Wembley, Neasden and Stanmore – then being developed by the extension of the Metropolitan Railway – but many others did not want to pull up their roots for the rather bleak rows of semis and shopping parades in the wilds of Middlesex, as they saw it.

Holidays were a very important and rather novel part of the young couple's life. The official one week a year paid holiday could be supplemented by an unpaid week which, allied to a free pass to Cleethorpes, Par or Ilfracombe and full board at £3 3s 0d a week, gave them a marvellous change from the brick canyons of the railway flats where the sun never penetrated. They became so attached to the annual holiday that in 1936 (when the author was born in June) they took it in October, by which time we could all travel the six hour journey to Cornwall. Promotion to passed fireman was more than cancelled out by the loss of mother's income and any hope of a suburban house was finished, but my father's transfer to Stratford in 1937 brought a more regular shift pattern. Life continued on a relatively even keel until the autumn of 1939 when evacuation of mother and son to Radlett soon after the declaration of war brought the first of many partings. A second child was on the way, the outer suburban natives decidedly hostile to the cockney invasion, although not to us personally, so with nothing much happening to London, we returned before Christmas.

Elsewhere on the system railwaymen were facing similar or worse hazards and long, uncertain hours with little prospect of improvement. They carried on with 'the one object of getting our trains safe to the end of the trip, and as near to time as possible', as a Stratford colleague of my father put it. Other hazardous areas included the south and east coast areas from Cornwall to the Borders where trains were liable to be machine-gunned by enemy aircraft, and where massed raids on Plymouth, Southampton and other centres disorganised services for days, although repairs were naturally made as soon as possible. Fortunately, in the days before the large-scale closures of the post-war era, there were always alternative routes. When the impossible was demanded railwaymen rose to the occasion. Over 600 extra trains from the Channel ports were run after Dunkirk as part of 'Operation Dynamo', other cavalcades evacuated whole cities, while each campaign demanded mass movement of men and material, culminating in the biggest operation of all – assembling everything under strictest secrecy for D-Day. Despite all the difficulties and shortages, it was made to happen.

Post-war days were almost an anti-climax. Times were still tough, with fuel shortages so acute that the council dug up wood-block road surfaces so that they could be sold as fuel and horse meat was supplied to supplement a totally inadequate ration for a heavy manual worker. But at least there was no bombing, and even better, summer holidays started again in 1947 with a return to Cornwall. My father's promotion to driver in 1948 and academic success for the family distinguished us from others where boys and girls were often in trouble. Movement to the suburbs by the better off started again, but father would only move around the corner to a four-roomed flat where he stayed until they were finally demolished in 1975, the last railwayman there, although by that time retired some five years.

Wharncliffe Gardens was a large urban microcosm of a working-class community. Similarities can be seen between it and other urban railway communities such as the Barracks at Peterborough, Hudson Town near Stratford and many others up and down the country. In common with the coal-mining and steel communities the railwaymen did shift work, but were more outward looking as they served the public much more directly. Many of their number travelled daily and brought back news of far places and other ways of life to their somewhat encapsulated wives and children, who nevertheless were able to shop, visit and be entertained in a more mixed environment. Rural railway communities on the other hand were more isolated, and the contrast between London railway flats and the terraced community grafted on to villages in the fastnesses of the shires is striking.

Woodford Halse was a largely railway community, set in the rural fastnesses of Northamptonshire, a junction on the Great Central's Sheffield to London main line, where a branch to Banbury connected that system to the Great Western, much used by coal and other goods trains as well as by cross-country passenger services. There was also a connection to the Stratford-upon-Avon & Midland Junction line, a single track cross-country line which had great aspirations but little traffic. The sleepy villages of Woodford and Hinton were more than adequately served by this line before the arrival of the line from the north in 1895. Terraces of housing were built in red brick, some of which were three-storey houses for families and railway lodgers. A new school, a much larger chapel, were built as well as a Tudoresque pub erected by the brewers, while the goods yard, locomotive depot and works supplied employment and wages on a scale not hitherto seen in that district.

The community that emerged was to last for seventy years, until the closure of the line in 1966. It continued to expand right up to the 1940s. Railwaymen bought the newer houses and a cinema was erected for their entertainment, a pleasant alternative to the Railway Institute in the days before television. Railway sons followed railway fathers, so there were no staffing problems even in the post-war period. The comparison with Neasden further south and the coalfield sheds which generated so much of the traffic was striking. As the farming community declined, the railwaymen became absolutely dominant. The little town was off major road routes, so lack of alternative activities meant that closure in 1966 stranded the community. Fortunately by this time car commuting allowed the younger and more active members of the town to travel to Banbury and Northampton, Rugby or Daventry, so the houses remained occupied. The older folk linger on, recalling their traditions and better days. The villages that became towns are like beached whales, uncertain of their future, proud of their past, but something precious was lost when railway communities were split up by rationalisation and closures in the 1960s.

Coping with problems was and still is a way of life for railwaymen. Decades of making do with antiquated equipment, buildings and supplies has inured them to getting on with the job under much less than perfect conditions and coming out in one piece if not exactly smiling. There has always been a large fund of goodwill and willingness to devote much more than basic time to getting the job right. Mutual Improvement Classes are an important illustration of this. Few other callings would mount Sunday morning voluntary classes for the benefit of those seeking promotion, staffed by those who had already passed their examinations. Likewise train crews skilled in first aid had learned their skills in voluntary classes of the St John Ambulance Brigade run in many railway settlements. These teams did consistently well in competitions against those from other callings and were of course invaluable in times of accident and war. Work-based leisure and community activities played a very large part in railway towns. Clubs, institutes and chapels specifically for the railway community allowed for their unsocial hours, so also tended to be the centres of such diverse activities as operatic and theatrical groups, allotment gardening, sports teams and much else. Many league soccer teams had their origins in railway sports clubs – Crewe Alexandra and Swindon Town being prominent – but there were at least half-a-dozen others.

Working, playing and living together had a major effect on the friendship patterns of the last generation of railwaymen. They regarded hierarchy and authority as normal, but remained friendly with promoted colleagues in general. Long-lasting friendships survived postings to distant parts of the system, aided by cheap travel and by an old-boy network that kept everybody informed of news and progress. Whether such patterns will survive the upheavals of cuts is a moot point, but the nature of the job, with the need for mutual aid and public service, indicates that it well might.

# 4
# Railway Works Towns

The most factory-like type of railway work was that offered by the great construction and repair shops maintained by pre-grouping railways. They were either newly established settlements such as Crewe, Eastleigh or Melton Constable or a newly built section of an existing town or city as at Derby, Ashford, Darlington or Glasgow. Here, and in a score of other centres up and down the country, a force of hundreds or thousands of workmen lived together as a railway settlement, their wives and children equally dominated by the works' hooter, the 'guv'nors' from locomotive superintendent to shop foreman, and by a system that controlled the whole pattern of their lives. The early work-force in such settlements was recruited from a number of sources, often millwrights and mechanics from industrial areas who saw opportunities for advancement in the new industrial towns set up by the railways. Later the resident railwaymen entered their sons for the better jobs through apprenticeship or influence with the foreman, leaving the labouring and less desirable jobs to the countrymen and hopeful migrants from other areas. A love-hate relationship with the company and the demands of the job developed. The tremendous pride in everything Great Western expressed by the author's Swindon relatives contrasted strongly with Alfred Williams' view that the great majority of the workmen 'loiter till the very last moment and spend not a second of time, more than they are absolutely bound, on company premises'.

The great railway workshops operated on a scale rarely seen in other industries until late in the nineteenth century. A large number of interdependent workshops grew up on a single site, calling for a large range of skills. As railways expanded and amalgamated during the nineteenth century and later, there was a tendency to concentrate work on major centres and close down or downgrade the minor works; thus Swindon expanded at the expense of Newton Abbot and Wolverhampton. The result was that by the second decade of this century literally thousands of workmen had to clock-in within a few minutes at Swindon and elsewhere as Alfred Williams so graphically described:

At ten minutes to six the hooter sounds a second time, then again at five minutes and finally at six o'clock. This time it makes a double report, in order that the men may be sure that it is the last hooter. Five minutes grace – from six till six-five – is allowed in the morning; after that everyone except clerks must lose time. As soon as the ten minutes hooter sounds the men come teeming out of the various parts of town in great numbers, and by five minutes to six the streets leading to the entrances are packed with a dense crowd of men and boys, old and young, bearded and beardless, some firm and upright, others bent and stooping, pale and haggard-looking, all off to the same daily toil and fully intent on the labour before them. It is a mystery where they all come from. Ten thousand workmen! They are like an army pressing forward to battle. Tramp! tramp! tramp! Still they pour down the streets, with the regularity of trained soldiers, quickening in pace as the time advances, until they come very near to the double and finally disappear through the entrances. Some of the young men's faces are ghastly white, very thin and emaciated, consumption very likely, while others are fresh and healthy looking.

Such a scene was repeated six days a week around the country at Horwich, Kilmarnock, Darlington, Brighton, Doncaster and Gorton. The endless toil of the heroic age of the Industrial Revolution lasted as long as the steam locomotive, although the hours were shortened after each world war. Hot metal, heavy weights and choking fumes were part of everyday life. Relatives with amputated fingers, crushed toes and seared skins were just outward signs of intolerable conditions in many shops within:

If the oil in the stampers' forges is worse than usual the dense clouds of nauseating smoke hang over you like a pall so thickly that you cannot see your fellows a few paces away, making it intensely difficult to breathe and adding a horrible disgust to the unspeakable weariness. Then the bright flashing metal and the white gas-jets show a dull red. Even the sound seems deadened by the smoke and stench, but this is merely the action of the impurity on the sense organs; they are so much impaired with the grossness of the atmosphere as to fail in their functions.

Although the pollution was known to kill, company doctors would have none of it. If a man could not stand it, there were always others who wanted his job.

The ten-hour day before 1919 meant ten hours of work, so that with time for lunch and breakfast, the worker was away from even a nearby home for a full twelve hours from Monday to Friday, but home by early afternoon on a Saturday. The heavy manual nature of the forge work meant that

ofttimes you would be quite lost, but the revolutions of the machine, the automatic strokes of the hammer, and the habit of the job control you. And if this should fail, your mate, half asleep, whacks his heat along and casts it upon your toe, or sears you with the hot tongs, or he misses the top of the tool at the anvil and strikes your thumb instead. There are many things that keep you alive, and always fear of not earning your money for the turn and having to be jeered at and bullied by the chargeman or overseer and so have your life made miserable.

After such a day, home in a two up, two down terraced house with screaming children, nagging wife and lodgers was enough to drive many to the pub for a few hours of respite before sleep and another start before dawn. Yet amid the heat, danger and stench the sensitive Alfred Williams was able to see beauty in

the faces and fronts of the smiths and forgers, as they stand at the fires or stoop over the metal, are brilliantly lit up – yellow and orange. Here are piles of finished forgings and stampings upon the ground – white, yellow, bright red, dull red, and almost black hot; the long tongues of fire leap up from the coke forges, and every now and then a livid sheet of flame bursts out of the stamper's dies. There is plenty of colour, as well as animation, in the picture, which obtains greater intensity through contrast with the blackness outside.

Boilermaking and riveting were deafening areas of the works, quite literally in the case of older employees. Crewe had its own steelworks on site, while brass and copper fittings were made in most works. Besides the heavy and dangerous work with metals, there was also a great deal of woodworking, lighter and pleasanter on both nose and eye. The carriage & wagon works were a normal adjunct of a locomotive works, a haven of relative peace and of low-key, high-quality craftsmanship, scented with exotic woods, varnish and paint.

Governing the conduct of the workshops was the rule book, administered often arbitrarily by the 'guv'nors', or 'gaffers' as they were often known. They were as detailed and thoroughgoing as anything that the operating staff had to follow. Punishments for quite minor offences appear draconian by present-day standards but were considered essential by those in authority. Some of the earliest rules to be framed were those at the Stockton & Darlington Railway's works at Shildon in 1833. They range from a fine of a shilling for using abusive language or swearing, to dismissal for drinking in working hours. By the middle of the nineteenth century the spread of railways and their attendant works meant that practices already established in pioneering areas filtered through to other parts of the country, bringing a new and harsh discipline to the rustics who started to work for the railways in places like Highbridge, Oswestry and Wolverton. There were also beneficial rules such as compulsory membership of sick funds and pension schemes.

Workmen were in charge of machinery worth considerable sums of money. A Crewe estimate was that each man had an average of £3,000 in capital in his charge, so consequently a whole list of offences relating to neglect or damage to machines was punishable by instant dismissal. They included inferior workmanship, improper use of machine, incorrect materials used, failing to clean machinery and removing borings and turnings with fingers rather than brushes. Lesser offences were fined an average of a day's wages. Even offences not deemed so gross were still the subject of a foreman's black list, a kind of

47

unofficial warning, putting the workman on probation – 'next time you're out'. Williams was probably overstating the case when he described the foreman's ideal as 'rough, ragged and round shouldered, a born fool, a toady and a liar, a tale-bearer, an indifferent workman – no matter what you are as long as you say "sir" to him, are servile and abject, see and hear nothing, and hold with him in everything he says and does: that is the way to get on in the factory'. Those terms would certainly not describe the many fine workmen the author has known who have 'got on', despite being bright, good at their job and holding strong religious and political opinions.

Despite the apparent harshness of the rule book there was flexibility in the operation of those rules. The foreman was the key figure in the railway workshops who negotiated the price of a job with the railway management almost as if he were an outside contractor. He also paid his men from the lump sum thereby gained in earlier days. Under those bowler hats and steely gazes there were crafty, calculating minds able to price keenly and negotiate cunningly, able to keep sound workmen relatively happy by granting an occasional privilege and by ignoring their occasional misdemeanour, while cracking down on agitators, apprentices and others caught in their web of disfavour. The foreman's 'blue-eyed boys' would clip a hedge, bring gifts of fruit and vegetables, or lean over the divide between the public and saloon bar in the pub to treat the gaffer to a pint, without trespassing in that preserve of the mighty or becoming over-familiar. The customs may have changed, but those seeking favour and promotion today use similar methods. Those like Alfred Williams who for conscience's sake refuse to bow, still remain unpopular.

Despite long hours, unpleasant conditions in some shops, varying degrees of tyranny by those in power and a great deal of regulation, railway towns were nevertheless much more attractive places to live in than most small industrial towns of the period or the largely unmodernised villages. For those who settled, work was more regular than in most occupations, while housing, amenities, education, holidays and welfare were decidedly superior to all but the best alternatives. Saltaire, Bournville and Port Sunlight had advantages over some railway towns, but they were the exceptions in manufacturing industry. Given the alternatives and the developing loyalty amongst those who had bettered themselves in railway towns, the 'railway family' in which successive generations entered the works, emerged during the nineteenth century. The railway connection in the Fuller family began when Ben Fuller senior started as a coppersmith at Ashford in 1847; his five sons entered the works and one of these had nine sons, all of whom entered the works, Ben junior rising to be foreman of grandfather's coppersmith shop and apprenticing his own son in post-war years as a coppersmith. Outsiders would stand little chance of making a start against such competition.

Those who did come from outside to work at Swindon were usually from the surrounding rural area. To maximise his chance of success, a man

> tidied himself up and, arrayed in clean working costume, presented himself at one of the main entrances immediately after breakfast time so as to meet the eyes of the foremen as they returned from the meal. Morning after morning, when work was plentiful, you might have seen a crowd of men and boys around the large doorways, or lining the pavement as the black army filed in, all anxious to obtain a job and looking wonderingly towards the opening in the dark tunnel through which the men passed to reach the different sheds . . . 'Chance of a job, sir?'. This was sometimes accompanied by an obsequious bow . . . If the foreman required any he asked them where they came from and what they were doing, and furthermore questioned them as to their age. If the answers were satisfactory he merely said 'Come along with me', and conducted the men off, and they followed with alacrity.

In this casual way the labouring and semi-skilled jobs were filled. The apprentices and the premium apprentices expected and got better. They were frequently from railway or middle-class families, had some secondary education and were expected to take higher grade posts after they were trained, right up to chief mechanical engineer or a comparable position in other engineering-related areas of the railway. Much of the training involved moving from job to job within the works, learning by 'sitting next to Nellie', supplemented with evening, or more recently day-release classes, in the railway institutes, originally set up by companies in towns such as Swindon, Crewe and even Melton Constable. Unless apprentices had a family or relatives in the town, they lodged with railway families, and whatever their background, they got their hands dirty stripping, assembling, repairing and turning, as well as learning draughtsmanship and design work on simple objects.

A Stratford apprentice who started in 1946 was one of the first not to have to pay a premium; indeed he was paid a few shillings a week from the start. In addition to the above duties he learned toolmaking, casting, welding and many other skills, largely taught by the older workmen. Post-war austerity and a steel shortage had compelled the application of great ingenuity to help to mitigate the chronic poverty of the LNER, forcing the works to patch up time-expired J15 locomotives half a century old and retyre carriage wheels that had been turning since Queen Victoria's day. The training was thorough, although apprentices tended to spend too long in parts of the works where labour was short and their low-paid services could be used to the full.

Today training is centred on Derby where British Rail Engineering take on 100 apprentices a year at sixteen years of age and then gives them three years of varied workshop experience with day-release classes in technical college. The BREL Training School monitors the programme so that the boys are not used for cheap labour and are rapidly rotated through a variety of skills. The labour-intensive railway equipment of former times has been largely discarded, so that a radically different type of training is given to a very much smaller body of apprentices.

A microcosm of a railway works town that has already been mentioned was Melton Constable, from 1881 until 1936 the hub of the Midland & Great Northern Joint Railway system. It was known facetiously as 'the Crewe of North Norfolk', but it did

Station staff, locomotive crew and platelayers at Hotwells (originally Clifton), terminus of the Bristol Port Railway & Pier Co's line from Avonmouth, which opened in 1865. The section between Sneyd Park and Hotwells was abandoned in 1922 and incorporated in the present road between Bristol and Avonmouth (*Locomotive & General Railway Photographs*)

Fireman Law and Driver Skinner on J15 No 65447 at Laxfield in 1952, about to take the mixed train at Haughley Junction (*Dr Ian C. Allen*)

Long service has been a notable characteristic of railway employment, a tribute to, and result of, the loyalty which the industry has generated. The author's father, Stan Joby (right), receives his gold watch on 9 May 1969 from F.D. Pattisson, Divisional Manager London, Western Region, at the Divisional Headquarters in Reading (*British Rail*)

everything from building a handful of locomotives (officially rebuilds to please Derby) down to repairing tarpaulins, in which latter capacity it dragged on an existence of sorts from 1936 until 1964 when the works and railway serving it finally closed. As with many other works towns, it was also an important junction and goods depot with the most important running shed on the M&GN system, so it is worthwhile examining the background to the town and, from memories of octogenarians, reconstructing a few days in the life of the town at its peak around 1911.

Two small railways were built from King's Lynn and Yarmouth towards Melton Constable opening in 1879 and 1877 respectively. The lines shared an office and a secretary in Yarmouth, were built simultaneously by the same firm of contractors, ordered similar locomotives and, from 1879, shared directors. None of these facts was coincidental, since one of the directors, Sir Edmund Lacon, admitted later that they had the object of building a line across Norfolk to join it to railways leading to the Midlands and the North.

The next problem was to join the two isolated lines together. Most of the land between Fakenham and North Walsham, the two temporary termini in north Norfolk was owned by Lord Hastings of Melton Constable Hall. He was very interested in bringing the line to join the sections across his land as it would raise its value, and if there were to be a line in any case, the more control that the landowner exercised, the more likely it was that it would be through points of his choosing. He also insisted on having the main junction and works of the system on his estate, a mere mile from Melton Constable Hall. A line was built from Melton Constable to Norwich, where it was welcomed by the shoemakers as competition for the Great Eastern. This was completed in 1882. Other lines were built to North Walsham in 1883 and to Cromer in 1887, severe financial difficulties halting construction of the latter for three years. Thus Melton Constable became the crossroads of Norfolk's second railway system and was given the nickname 'the Crewe of North Norfolk'.

A ruined church, a farm and fields were all that was to be

found in the northern corner of Melton Constable parish before 1881. The site was hardly a natural choice for a major railway junction, being almost the highest point in the county. However, the help from Lord Hastings, both in land and in the House of Lords, was invaluable, so it was prudent to allow him to determine the site. How much coal and fireman's sweat was later wasted on this steep climb to Melton Constable from all directions can never be estimated, but it must have been considerable. A small works was set up and a row of terraced houses, Melton Street, was built. They were just over a mile from the large existing village of Briston. Shortly after the establishment of the railway colony, a young engineer, William Marriott, arrived to take charge of the handful of locomotives and of construction; he was to dominate the village for the next forty years.

The first few years of the system were a mighty struggle for mere survival. In 1883 the line had changed its name from that of the constituent small local lines to the ambitious but untrue Eastern & Midlands Railway. It had large plans but very little money. Its manager, Robert Read, was adept at raising money and obtaining stock and materials before a penny changed hands. He had had a lot of practice at this, running a very similar ramshackle railway in the West Country between Bath and Bournemouth – the Somerset & Dorset. Although the E&MR was largely built by 1883, it had to attract traffic which was not easy in what was a period of depression, especially since the Great Eastern Railway was understandably hostile to this interloper. Only half the intended lines were built. Neither the extension from Norwich to Dereham, nor that across the Broads to Martham, nor the north coast line from Kelling to Blakeney and Wells were even started. By 1887 insufficient money was coming in to pay for maintenance and wages, let alone for new lines, new equipment and the mounting sum of interest on loans. Since the latter were not paid, the railway went into receivership with a view to early sale.

Melton Constable's first few years were very tough indeed.

Railwaymen were recruited from other railways and from farming jobs, then brought to what was described as 'a godforsaken spot' where they lived in cramped conditions in unfamiliar town-type houses with no shops, no entertainments other than those they could provide for themselves, no school, and until the Hastings Arms was built, no pub either. Turnover of labour was high in the first few years. The jobs at Melton Constable were to drive and fire the locomotives, repair and maintain rolling stock and track, and to man the station and the passenger and goods trains. The two terraces of Melton Street were not enough to accommodate such a large body of workers, so in 1886, a third terrace, Astley Terrace was built. This was erected by a local builder on a promise from William Marriott to guarantee the rent of 1/6d per week for each house. Staff who rented these houses had to take up to four lodgers nominated by the railway company as a matter of course, making the houses very overcrowded at times. Other workers rented previously empty houses in surrounding villages such as Briston and Hindolvestone. By 1891, there was not an empty house for miles around, a rare occurrence in rural Norfolk in the late Victorian period. About 600 people in and around Melton Constable depended on the railway for their livelihood by that time, an island of industry in a rather bucolic sea of depressed agriculture.

Despite its poverty, the Eastern & Midlands Railway put on a brave show. Its shiny engines and immaculate stations of neat architectural appearance were noted by the leisure press of the period. It offered through connections from many points in Norfolk to London and the Midlands. Robert Read worked very hard to sell the line to interested parties and to this end projected its image as a going concern that only needed more capital and an upturn in the national economy to flourish. He also wanted to bale out the shareholders who had been without dividends, often from the start of operations. The Great Eastern Railway was not at all interested, as the lines were either competitive with its existing lines or formed poor connections with its own routes. The Great Northern Railway and the Midland Railway were much more alive to the possibilities, seeing in the expansion of resorts and the movement of produce ways of increasing their own traffic. They eventually took over the Eastern & Midlands in 1893 as a joint concern, each owning 50 per cent of the capital.

The poverty of the previous decade was immediately apparent to the engineers of the new parent companies, who recommended relaying large sections of the track and ordered large numbers of locomotives, coaches and wagons, both to replace the worst of what there was, and also to prepare for the deluge of traffic that the parent companies were to pour on to their new acquisition. A direct connection from the western end of the system to Leicester was built, making for easy running through to the Midlands. As a result, cuts of up to two hours were possible in the timetables of long-distance expresses in the late 1890s. The increased capacity also permitted the running of dozens of excursion trains, which became a feature of the Edwardians summer season. It was possible to make the return trip from King's Cross to Yarmouth via Peterborough and Melton Constable for 4/-, but it was just as well that few of the clients could read maps! All possible traffic from the Midlands and the North was pushed onto the system, and maximum publicity was relayed through the press to make sure that the public heard about the wonders of a Norfolk holiday.

Melton Constable benefited greatly from these changes. New houses of a much higher standard were erected on the south side of Briston Road and also forming the new Colville Road, named after a director of the Great Northern Railway. The houses were made of Fletton bricks rather than local Norfolk Reds, with slated roofs, damp courses, running water, toilets and even bow windows. In the settlement itself, Colman's the grocers set up, the Railway Institute was erected in brick and then enlarged, the primary school and later the secondary school opened to cope with the local baby boom, while on the servicing of the community, the gasworks and waterworks were greatly enlarged to cope with increased demand. Likewise the engineering shops and locomotive shed grew in scale, the former being so well equipped that it could erect locomotives by the early years of this century. Melton Constable even had a market in the first decade of the twentieth century.

The busiest days in the year for the little railway community were summer Saturdays, when over a hundred trains moved through the junction from the early hours of the morning until well into the early hours of Sunday morning, connecting the resorts of Norfolk with London and the cities of the East Midlands and even further afield.

In the still of the night, the most active place was the engine shed, where some thirty engines had to be prepared for the coming rush. A few gas lights in the yard and the nearby station lit up polished highlights of the gorse-coloured paintwork and brasswork on the elegant little engines quietly hissing outside the shed. The greenish glare and the long black shadows gave an air of mystery to the cleaning lads who brought kindling and oily waste down the stationary rows of polished engines, tossing it up on to the footplate of each in turn. The rasp of shovel on coal and metal told of engines being lit up, while a dribble of thick, choking smoke from some chimneys and the glimpse of a dull red glow between driving wheels indicated that some were more advanced than others in their steam-raising. The early hours of Saturday mornings were no time for card schools inside fireboxes or practical jokes; work was against the clock for the next twenty-four hours and more. The dawn slowly illuminating the dense pall of smoke inside the shed and the signal gantry on the Norwich line warned the lads detailed to knock up sleeping engine crews that their task was approaching, and that they had better finish off their present duties to the satisfaction of the chargeman.

Just before 4.00am a group of lads scurried across the platform from the engine shed and then fanned out to hammer at the doors of sleeping drivers. If the first tattoo did not have the desired effect, then a handful of gravel directed at the bedroom window was tried, followed by more hammering, until a sleep-drugged curse or missile from a raised window showed evidence of mission accomplished. It was always a problem to know who to wake first when there was a group. It was probably safest to start with the one with the sweetest temper, hoping that the progressing din would have started to arouse those called later. The lads returned to their labours, checking each firebox to see that all was well and adding coal judiciously. As the light strengthened, drivers and firemen started to arrive, climbing aboard their allotted engines to check that all was well and that steam pressure was increasing. The rattle of coal in the tenders increased in frequency as firemen made up their fires to their liking, thin and hot. The drivers pottered around with their oil cans, filling oil reservoirs, looking for signs of wear. Then it was a matter of taking one's turn in the queue for water and coal, cleaning up the footplate afterwards, giving the metalwork a polish and re-reading instructions before setting down to await an outward train.

The works staff had cursed the shed lads in their half-sleep at dawn, but their turn came to get up after 5.00am. Back-yard chickens and pigs added to the general stirring as the sun crept higher. By 5.45am, doors were beginning to slam as flat-capped men sauntered along Melton Street and Briston Road, over the bridge and down the steep flight of steps into the works. As the time for the hooter neared, steps became faster, until the last were almost frantic, running the last few yards to the time clock, so as to avoid a swingeing fine for lateness.

The 'slap-slap' of the drive belts coming down from the squeaking drive-shafts, the clanging of metal on metal, showers of sparks from grinding wheels and the whirr of the overhead crane overcame the clanking, whistling and banging from outside. For the next couple of hours, tasks unfinished from Friday or new tasks were tackled. The gaffers strolled round, eyes, nose and ears at the ready to detect any breach of rules, but usually little was wrong. The machinery was new, the community much smaller and closer than those at Crewe or Swindon. Some 300 men did every job from painting to erection between them. Until 8.15am work progressed at an even tenor;

then there was a blast of the hooter and three-quarters of an hour in the canteen, where boxes of bread, cheese, onions and bottles of cold tea would relieve the pangs of hunger. Work finished at 1.00pm on Saturday, so it was back to work with a will at the 9.00am hooter for the last session of the week.

When the final works' hooter of the week blew at 1.00pm, the machines received their last wipe, the apprentices put their oil cans down and the carpenters in the carriage shop neatly shelved their planes and chisels. It was freedom for a precious day and a half. Like the workmen, the office staff had Saturday afternoons off, but some could be called on to help with paperwork in the station when staff were at breaking point.

In the offices at the east end of the works, William Marriott oversaw all. He was the respected chief of the M&GN clan who, by the end of the Edwardian era, had been in charge of Melton Constable for nearly thirty years. He was a God-fearing man of high principles and had a great sense of status. Once when a junior clerk was asked to nip up to the drawing office to see if the fire was in order just before Marriott was expected, the junior found that it needed attention, which he was giving it when Marriott walked in. He was told to desist, as fires were the head messenger's job! As a chapel man, he expected his flock to attend service, but there were both churchmen and men of no church on the staff, so he did not always have his own way. He trained his apprentices thoroughly, teaching them to make the immaculate drawings for which he was famous, giving them a grounding of a breadth that could only be accomplished in a works where everybody knew everybody else.

William Marriott's office overlooked the engine shed and station, both the busiest on the M&GN system. Coal economy was a fetish with him, as was the single-heading of even the heaviest trains. A league table of coal usage was posted for all to see, as well as being recorded in the minute book. The thin, white-hot fire was an M&GN characteristic, taught to all new firemen, and observed unless they wished to incur the Marriott wrath. With it, fourteen coaches were hauled across Norfolk, unassisted on banks, to be handed over to a brace of Midland engines of more recent vintage at South Lynn or Bourne. Yet the engines were not flogged mercilessly to death, as were those black engines on the LNWR; they lasted well – the original Beyer Peacock 4-4-0s of 1882 were the oldest 4-4-0s on the LNER when that company took over the M&GN in 1936.

In the village itself, Saturday was the main shopping day. Early trains from the coast brought up fish and shellfish hawkers, who did a brisk house-to-house trade following pay-day. Dripping wickerwork baskets contained the night's catch from the Sheringham boats. The children, free of school, got their ha'penny gobstoppers or everlasting chews from Colman's after mother had reeled off her long list of groceries. Food for the family and the lodgers made shopping a lengthy business. Men coming in from a distance stayed overnight with local families, as did single men who needed a bed. Many of the jobs required them to be within minutes of the station, shed or works, so lodging in distant villages was impossible.

After the midday meal, there was work to be done on the allotments, mucking out of livestock or gardening for the works men. A highlight of this smallholding tradition was pig-killing, a spectacle enjoyed by many, young and old alike. The results were shared out between the neighbours, right down to the black pudding and trotters. The brass band often had local engagements on the Saturday afternoon, squeezing aboard a train to an outlying village. The bowling green at the end of Melton Street was much used, but if there was a wedding on, the game gave way to the reception and photographs by tradition. The green was overlooked by a bay where engines awaited their trains, and legend has it that if the railway team was losing, the driver would obligingly send up a shower of cinders from the chimney, which would descend on the green and give a rough ride to the visiting team's bowls.

By mid-afternoon the flow of traffic was predominantly towards the seaside. Long-stay holidaymakers going on holiday replaced the excursionists and returning holidaymakers. They gave the refreshment-room staff a badly needed respite, as they usually still had the remains of picnic baskets brought from home. After a wedding, the 4.08pm was the favourite departure. The guard would be warned to keep a compartment locked until Melton Constable. The happy couple were seen aboard with much ceremony, and then the train departed to the explosions of fog signals according to a code never mentioned in the rule book. Further explosions at intermediate points could be expected, as the signalmen telegraphed the happy news along the line.

At dusk, windows lit up with gas mantles. Tea, as the evening meal is called in Norfolk, was late on Saturdays in summer. Men from the works had finished their gardening or sport and the children had come in from the fields and lanes. Jugs of fresh milk had been brought up from the dairy down the Brinton lane, as all was being readied for the day of rest. Not all would partake of rest, especially if traffic was heavy, but the Gospel Hall was always full, while the local church choir would not have existed but for railwaymen and their wives and daughters. A spelling competition called a spelling-bee at the Railway Institute, a quiet pint and skittles at the Hastings Arms offered relaxation, while talk turned to plans for the annual outing for the children to Cromer on a flag-bedecked train with William Marriott playing uncle to his extended family of over 1,000 employees and their families. The annual shut down of the works for a week also gave families the opportunity of returning to other parts of the country, whence so many of them had come as recruits to the railway in its younger days.

Modest in size though it was, Melton Constable provided a full range of services to its small isolated system in the same way as Crewe, Eastleigh, Doncaster and many others did to their own larger systems. The communities of railway towns were often distant from other large centres, lacked good road connections until well into the twentieth century and were slow to acquire alternative sources of employment; indeed, the companies were hostile to the loss of their monopoly over the work-force, as paternalists often are.

The established railway families in these towns became the local working-class establishment. They were the councillors, mayors when there was no suitable management candidate, church sidesmen, secretaries of societies and later of unions when these became respectable. So long as they played their cards right, there would be apprenticeships, clerical posts or manual positions for their sons, who would have grown up in railway houses situated in streets named after directors or engineers. The sons had railway relatives and were educated in a school endowed by the railway, as a plate mounted above the entrance would remind them. Railway holiday trains took them to resorts where hundreds of their townsfolk would spend a week or fortnight simultaneously. Should misfortune strike the family, the railway-subsidised provident fund would help out and railway orphanages provided a long stop should relatives be unable to help a bereaved family. In such an atmosphere conformity was at a premium, or as a foreman was heard to say to a new boy, 'Keep yer nose clean and yer'll be all right like yer Dad'.

Those who did not conform, were merely different or known troublemakers, had a hard time of it as Alfred Williams at Swindon frequently found to his cost. As a writer whose horizons extended well beyond the pub, allotments, Swindon Town football club and the institute, he did not fit in. His perspectives and feelings were thus very different from those whose bow-windowed 'gaffers houses' in the same Swindon represented security, warmth and a comfortable, predictable future for themselves and their offspring. They were proud of the GWR and enforced its ways on the nonconformists. This unfortunately sometimes took the form of victimisation when labour had to be shed. Slumps and strikes resulted in management asking each department to produce lists of men to be made redundant. Not surprisingly this often included those who did not fit in or who had been agitating for improvements that the company was not prepared to make. Since their skills were often only marketable in railway towns and they had been discharged or even blacklisted, there was little to be gained from migrating to Doncaster from Swindon where there was also likely to be a dearth of work. They drifted away, few knew where.

It is to the credit of the railway companies in the inter-war period that they encouraged other companies to set up works in railway towns. Rolls-Royce in Derby and Crewe, and Pressed Steel and Imperial Tobacco in Swindon, provided alternative employment at a time when the railways were making many employees redundant, thus averting what could have been a disastrous situation in the depression years. The monopoly of power held by the company's representative on the shopfloor slipped as alternatives became available, but it took another war and full employment to destroy the old discipline and usher in an age when the railways actively had to seek staff and could not afford to lose skilled men.

# 5

# *Train Crews*

For more than a century the desire of every boy who joined the railways as a cleaner was supposed to be to become an engine driver. Airline pilot or even spaceman has probably superseded such desires in recent years for those going into transport. For those unable to aim at the footplate, a porter could get on the move by being promoted to guard. This desire for movement, control and status, even of a smart military-style uniform in the case of the guard, has made the role of train crews an enviable one and propelled many youths into starting a career with prospects of joining such crews, despite the hard work and hazards along the way, the strong likelihood of failing long before reaching the coveted job, and the irregular hours, shift work and dirt that went with the work.

The first regularly employed railway locomotive enginemen, as they were then called, were Robert Morrow and James Stephenson, who worked for the Stockton & Darlington Railway in February 1826 for 3/8d per day, changed to ¼d per ton per mile, to include payment of fireman's and assistants' wages, coal, lubricants and other necessities of *Locomotion*, No 1, and its kind. The idea was to make the enginemen economy conscious, but also they were apparently not averse to borrowing part of their load when on the move. Whether this was repaid was open to doubt. The opening of the Liverpool & Manchester Railway, colliery lines strong enough to bear steam engines and the later growth of passenger-carrying lines in many parts of the country, made it necessary to find acceptable men who were fit, mechanically competent and who could run their little engines in a disciplined way, keeping to a schedule and obeying instructions.

The harum-scarum days of coaching were not a good precedent. Drastic punishments were meted out to those who did not take care of their steeds, but enginemen had a premium rating, so they could obtain another post, sometimes as strike-breakers. Those in steady jobs also received tempting offers from newly opened lines, a situation against which the Liverpool & Manchester guarded by instituting lengthy notice periods for resigning drivers.

Just how crude the early running of trains was, is summarised in a contemporary book first published in 1852, *Our Iron Roads*, by F. S. Williams who was the historian of the Midland Railway. The trains of which he wrote were braked only by the locomotive and by the guard in his brake van. They needed to work the train as a team, whether it was goods or passenger, so a system of whistles between the two was devised. The engine driver blew short, sharp whistles, the guard deep-toned ones. Half a mile after starting a goods train, driver and guard exchanged whistles, then every two miles. With passenger trains, every mile was recommended. In an emergency the guard was to apply the brake suddenly and then quickly release it. The qualities looked for in train crews were 'intelligence, activity and watchfulness', while civility for those with passenger duties was also considered very important. The picture that Williams gave of early engine drivers on their unprotected footplates was similar to that of the romanticised sailor, who has

To bear the pelting brunt of the tempestuous night,
With half-shut eyes, and pucker'd cheeks, and teeth
Presented bare against the storm.

Williams himself experienced the wild rocking of the footplate and marvelled at the toughness of those who worked under such hard conditions.

In the days before continuous brakes became common on the railways in the 1880s, it was very difficult to stop trains under wet or greasy conditions. On 10 September 1881 a Massey Bromley 0-4-4T of the Great Eastern Railway was working a train of thirteen vehicles, all small light carriages of the period, with a front and rear brake van, from North Walsham to Cromer. Only one brake van was manned, a new 12 ton vehicle which was considered by the guard and North Walsham stationmaster to be adequate, but in drizzling rain and with greasy rails the engine skidded past Cromer signal box at 5mph. The driver jumped down, shovelling ballast on the rails and in the end jammed his shovel under the wheels of the engine but to no avail. The engine went sailing into two empty carriages at the buffer stops, knocking down the porters' shed and damaging two of the train vehicles. Two guards should have been on the train, and the Westinghouse engine brake applied earlier. It stressed the need for good continuous brakes.

The train crews who had the most glamorous jobs were those on express passenger trains. They worked largely by day, earned the best money, and in former times were even provided with better uniforms. Goods traffic in the opinion of many was much more demanding as the trains were primitively braked until very recently, conditions were rough on the footplate and in the guard's van, while the co-ordination required between members of the crew was of the highest order. When this co-ordination broke down under difficult conditions, the results could be most unpleasant, as evidenced on the Brecon & Merthyr Railway at Torpantau Tunnel on the precipitous line across the Brecon Beacons. Three tank engines were used to haul unbraked freight trains, and the greatest dread was of trains getting out of control on the down gradient:

Evidence of Thomas Meyrick, guard:
I am a goods guard in the service of the B&MR Company. I was on the train that met with the accident. I arrived at Torpantau about nine o'clock that night, and started about 9-10pm. After one of the engines had taken water, I believe it was the fireman Joseph Davies said 'Are you right, Tom?'. I replied 'All right' and we started away. I pinned down as many breaks [sic] as possible on my side. When we had entered the tunnel the last engine whistled and when we got to the north end I told my mate to look after the van break, and I got out and rode on the waggons half way down the bank. The van then began to roll, and the train was going speed, I thought. The next thing I

recollect was being in bed at the White Hart.

We are supposed according to instructions to stop at the north end of the tunnel, but we did not do so. When we came out of the north end of the tunnel, the breaksman, my mate, showed the red light to stop to the front engines, upon which were Joseph Thomas and Thomas Williams as drivers. But they did not stop. I put some of the breaks down as we were travelling. The speed increased most rapidly after passing the fir plantation. I do not remember speaking to my mate after returning to the van. I am quite sure that there was not one man on the train under the influence of drink. It was not a heavy train. The tunnel was full of steam as we went through. If we think we have enough breaks down we do not give the signal to stop, but when we have three engines we generally do so. We went sharply through the tunnel. Every break ought to be put down, but we do not always do so. I have only once in two years run wild so far as the river bridge at Talybont.

The vision of guard and brakesman hopping on and off the van, running alongside the accelerating train on a wet stormy night, pinning down stiff brake levers while trying to keep the double-headed train under control and the banking engine informed of progress, is quite terrifying. Even passenger trains were largely braked manually by the guard in the late 1870s, adding to the hazards of travel at a time when traffic was increasing markedly. Some new railways were built as a result of this increase, poorly capitalised and evidently run on the cheap, for example by expecting their men to work around the clock. This was certainly the case with the Midland & South Western Junction Railway in 1891 when guard James Choules died tragically in the station yard at Weyhill, near Andover.

Weyhill Fair had just finished, increasing the volume of traffic on the line. The porter at Weyhill, Edward Pike, had been on duty since 9.00am, the night was wet and windy, trains were running late and Pike stayed on duty into the early hours of the next morning. A pick-up goods train, hours late, threaded its way into the yard, driven by William Annalls who had been in service with the MSWJR for only two months after four years with the LSWR. He arrived at Weyhill at 3.08am. Choules came forward to say that there was something to pick up:

I set back till clear of the siding points and was then uncoupled and went forward ahead of the siding points. When I knocked the first truck back I ran a little further than was necessary, being unable to stop my engine on slippery rails. I applied a little steam to start, but shut it off again and my fireman applied the brake. It was so dark that I cannot say exactly how far I followed the loose truck but I must have run very close to it. I did not hear it strike the empty wagon on the sidings, and I did not feel anything to indicate that I had struck the loose truck a second time. I did not see any lamp after I was called back [he continued shunting] . . . As soon as I came to a stand porter Pike called to me from the ground. He called 'Come down here Bill a minute, look sharp!' I jumped off and found that Pike had Choules in his arms. Choules was breathing but unconscious. He had been uncoupling between two wagons and was pinched between the buffers.

Further enquiry revealed that Choules had been on duty for 22 hours 18 minutes at the time of the accident and the driver for a similar time. The foreman at Swindon had earlier offered the driver relief there, but he was anxious to return to his home in Andover for his off-duty day. He added in mitigation that, 'I have been on duty before this for 24 hours at a time, but owing to exceptional causes'. James Tyrell, the locomotive foreman at Swindon added, 'I have had no complaints from my men as to overtime'. Investigation of the time book of guard Norris on the same line revealed duty on successive days of 20 hours 50 minutes, 20 hours 29 minutes, 19 hours, 18 hours 15 minutes, 18 hours 15 minutes and 18 hours 10 minutes. Long single line sections and staff shortage were blamed for this appalling state of affairs, which led Major Marindin of the Board of Trade to recommend a maximum of 10 hours in future to avoid overtired men putting themselves and the public at grave risk. Guard Choules did not die in vain.

The pattern of training for enginemen evolved by the middle of the nineteenth century: one of doing menial jobs while learning. From cleaning to firing and then to driving could take some thirty years, while top-link work, until the last days of steam, was rare until a man was well into his fifties. There was also much relevance in the phrase 'many are called but few are chosen'. Of the many youngsters who donned overalls to become cleaners, perhaps a quarter would stay in the running department and eventually become drivers. Eyesight, physical fitness, the ability to maintain a clean record in a hazardous occupation, the sheer stamina of working 12, then 10 and latterly 8 hour shifts, often with overtime, in all weathers, demanded so much of a man that many gave up long before their hand could regularly rest on the regulator.

The instincts and feel for the job that a footplateman acquires were noted by a nineteenth-century locomotive inspector as being: 'The ear should be trained to detect, on the footplate, the slightest variation in the beat, so that if four carriages out of the sixteen were to become detached through a coupling breaking, it would be known on the footplate instantly'. Thus spoke the practical man whose experience was learned in the harsh conditions of the open footplate and never-ending working day of the 1860s. Another observer, F. S. Williams, noted that enginemen

form an important and intelligent class, who have arisen under the exigencies of the times to an arduous post, but one which leads them to be overlooked by the community in general. The great responsibilities devolving on the engine-men and firemen of our railways, demand that their personal qualifications should be unexceptionable, as to their sobriety, activity, vigilance, and presence of mind.

The same, in somewhat less purple prose, could be said to be the requirements up to the present day. By a process of elimination, the railways acquired just such a body of men. The railway companies took on far more youngsters than they could possibly promote later, thereby obtaining a cheap labour force to do the mucky jobs about the shed, amid the ash, oil, coal dust and soot. Those who survived their initiation were likely to become railwaymen to the core.

The career patterns of two drivers are instructive in showing both changes and lack of them for those who started in 1922 and 1946 respectively. Both started in their mid-teens after a world war, but the contrasts in social conditions meant that promotion was much faster in the 1940s. In World War I, if one passed an examination in literacy and numeracy, one could leave school, an option often taken by poor families who needed an extra wage, however small. For the next five years my father, the first example, worked first as a bench hand with Desoutters, the engineers who were making munitions at that time. He was so small that he had to stand on a box to reach the work-bench. There followed a period as a tea boy in Grove Road power station, opposite Wharncliffe Gardens, and then a very unhappy period as a football apprentice with Queens Park Rangers, from which he was bought out. By the age of seventeen a number of other careers became available, including the police and the railways. The former did not appeal, but the railways were already familiar. His elder brother Charlie had been a fireman on the Metropolitan Railway since 1905, many of the neighbours were on the railways, so when a vacancy occurred at Neasden shed, he applied and was taken on as a probationer.

The railways had the pick of the teenage boys who wanted a secure job in the early 1920s. There were fewer opportunities in most other industries in the aftermath of a war which robbed Britain of many overseas markets. The consumer industries of the 1930s had yet to develop. Stiff medicals, poor starting wages and rough conditions on shift work failed to deter large numbers of lads from applying. The generation ahead of this post-war bulge had benefitted from fast promotion in wartime, and with returned servicemen they created a promotion block which lasted until World War II. Promotion became a very slow crawl up a greasy pole, even in the relatively prosperous London area, so that my father was forty-three years of age before he became a driver.

Neasden in 1922 was one of the newest and smartest of the locomotive depots around London, home to beautifully maintained green engines which were often larger than those of other depots nearby, such as Cricklewood and Willesden, and very much larger than those across the line at the Metropolitan depot where his brother worked. Cleaning the locomotives could be rewarding in more senses than one. The joy of bringing the Great Central livery to perfection before the engine backed down to Marylebone to take out a Manchester express was added to by the habit of some drivers tipping the cleaners a tanner to emery-paper the buffers into quadrants to give them that final touch of excellence. There were also the dirty jobs: using prickers and bent darts to service the firebox, clean caked oil and coal-dust out of the inside valve motion under impossibly cramped conditions were all part of the day's and night's work. At the end of a day shift, a good soaking in the tin tub before the black-leaded range was a vital prelude to escorting my mother out for the evening. On pay of under £1 a week, marriage was out of the question, but they still seemed to go out a lot – films, concerts and amateur football for my father.

The General Strike of 1926 was the first watershed in my father's career. Like most of his mates in ASLEF, my father went on strike. Those who did not were marked men for the rest of their careers. When the strike collapsed less than a fortnight later, the company took back men only as needed. The coal strike in Nottinghamshire and elsewhere continued, thus limiting Great Central traffic to a trickle on the goods side. The result was a layoff of six months, spent happily enough travelling, courting and odd-jobbing, but on returning to Neasden in the late autumn it was evident that a move was necessary if his career was to progress.

King's Cross wanted passed cleaners and firemen in 1927, so my father, together with Bill Hoole and several others, started work at 'Top Shed', away from semi-rural Neasden. There was a noticeable coolness on the part of the King's Cross drivers towards their new firemen. Many of the drivers had worked through the General Strike and they also resented the standard-isation of working conditions that the LNER brought in, which they thought were inferior to those of the old Great Northern. So although he learned his craft at King's Cross, was able to marry on a fireman's wage, and had a pleasant life outside work hours, King's Cross did not provide my father's pleasantest memory.

A decade after moving to King's Cross came another move, this time to Stratford, which is dealt with in the chapter on the goods yard at Devonshire Street. In 1948, my father's career came full circle, with a return to Neasden as a driver. The work at Devonshire Street, shunting in a confined goods yard as a passed fireman, was not a good preparation for the range of work at Neasden, but Neasden was a very different shed from what it had been in the days just after the grouping. Now a factory-lined North Circular Road dominated the shed, surrounded by suburbia. Jobs were plentiful, so the dingy, run-down locomotive depot had the greatest difficulty in obtaining and retaining staff to do the dirtier jobs. To add to the problems, Neasden was nobody's baby. It was too far west to fit into the Eastern Region, while the main line that it served was largely in the London Midland Region, yet Marylebone and Neasden spent some years in the Western Region. Despite the problems, shedmaster Bill Harvey and his successors strove manfully to run a good service, which was always under the eagle eye of management, as the headquarters of the new British Railways was just across the road from Marylebone station.

Post-war London was a mecca for provincial firemen who were aiming at the top link. Young men from Norwich, Truro, Aberystwyth, Inverness and points in between were drawn to the undermanned sheds of the great city where plentiful overtime and fast promotion, not to mention entertainment and freedom from the constraints of home, beckoned invitingly to the ambitious. With nationalisation, inter-regional transfers became possible, so Bill Harvey and other shedmasters in the provinces found that they were losing their most go-ahead passed cleaners and firemen, who would rough it in London for a few years, rise in the service and then return home when a vacancy arose, often promoted ahead of older colleagues who had not moved. Yet there were many drawbacks in the career of the young man who went to London. Railway hostels were few and usually full, while most landladies did not want oily boots and greasy overalls marking their highly polished floors and furnishings. The hours worked ensured that railway lodgers would disturb every other lodger nightly and often at weekends as well, so some aspirants to the regulator found themselves sleeping in old air-raid shelters, or in the multi-bedded dosshouses of Camden Town and Islington along with muddy construction workers, feeding largely on Irish stew, bread and marge and drinking copious mugs of thick tea.

To these brisk young hopefuls were added the immigrants who started to arrive in large numbers in the late 1940s. Anglo-Indians from the railway system of the sub-continent were well trained in British ways, although not always happy in the lower grade jobs that they were given. The Ukranian cleaning squad at Top Shed, King's Cross, were highly successful in turning out Pacifics with a pre-war sheen. Elsewhere, language, attitudes and cultures clashed from time to time. Dark tales came from grimy, shabby sheds like Neasden and Stratford of engines abandoned by firemen and even of fights on the footplate where drivers tried to enforce traditional discipline on a recalcitrant recruit. The worst situations developed when sulky firemen were paired with drivers downgraded to empty stock workings or shunting for poor timekeeping or culpable accidents. With plenty of jobs available elsewhere and no lifelong commitment to railways, many of the new recruits did not respond in a conventional way, much to the alarm of the driver. To some of the older men, redundancy or conversion to single-manning in electric or diesel trains came as a welcome relief.

Meanwhile, most drivers coped with bad coal, poor maintenance and varied mates as best they could. At Neasden the main traffic was to the Chilterns for both British Railways and for the Metropolitan from Rickmansworth northwards. The coal trains ran like a conveyor belt southwards, some ending up in the Marylebone power station or in the coalyard nearby. Half-a-dozen expresses for Manchester and one to Bradford were shared with Leicester depot, so there was little hope of that work for a newcomer. Other traffic was introduced in order to make more use of the Great Central main line; the Starlight Specials and the

Bletchley parcels trains via the Calvert Loop were examples. Locomotive power was usually adequate, although a few Great Central tank engines were still used, a reminder of early days.

A favourite turn was the Chesham branch push-and-pull train. A former Great Central 4-4-2T was coupled to some original Metropolitan Railway electric stock and this odd combination ran up and down the curvaceous wooded branch line all day. In the middle of the day, the crew were scarcely bothered by passengers, so could take the opportunity of stopping the train to pick horseradish, a delicacy beloved by my father, which grew abundantly on some cutting slopes.

The ASLEF strike of drivers and firemen in 1955 probably did more than any other event to point out that the nation could manage quite well without the railways. Thereafter certain lines were singled out for a run-down of services which were duplicated by others. The Great Central was one of these, together with the M&GN and western parts of the LSWR lines. The express services from Marylebone were not developed and in 1959 they were largely axed, while the dieselisation of the suburban services meant that there was a surplus of footplate staff at Neasden. The announcement of the electrification of the Metropolitan lines to Amersham and Chesham indicated that the writing was on the wall for Neasden depot. Footplate staff were offered the choice of registering with Cricklewood motive power depot of the London Midland Region, staying on at Neasden until no longer required, or transferring to the Western Region, once in charge of Neasden and over whose lines many of the suburban trains still ran. At Old Oak Common, the training programme for conversion to diesel locomotives had created vacancies. Family conferences were held. Swindon relatives thought that there was expansion on the Western Region, while other relatives who were drivers at Cricklewood did not see much future in the coal traffic. The matter was decided on the final day for application when my mother put father's grease cap on his head, helped him into his donkey jacket and told him not to come back until he had signed on for the Western Region. We had always gone west for our holidays, so that finished the argument.

Old Oak Common was a revelation after Neasden. The depression of Neasden lifted, we heard no more about firemen who were useless. That final renaissance of Western steam was under way and father was part of it! Several weeks were spent learning the new roads, differences in signalling, automatic train control, the slightly strange controls, all noted down in immaculate copperplate in a little pocket notebook. The sparkling paintwork, brass and copper plus the enthusiasm of young West Country and Welsh firemen gave driving a new lease of life. Every detail of the track and line-side points of reference were noted. The approaches to stations were particularly important. An overbridge was a good reverberator of exhaust on the approach to Pewsey, a signal to apply the brake slowly for a smooth halt, the pointwork at Aynho was a similar trigger on the approaches to Banbury.

Old Oak Common shed served more individual main lines out of London than did any other motive power depot. Wolverhampton, Worcester, South Wales, Bristol and Plymouth were all learned over the next five years, interspersed by long periods of relieving on all manner of trains from expresses to parcels and milk trains. At home we learned that a 'double-home Plymouth' did wonders for father's pay packet, while on some relief turns, whist in the mess-room paid for the rent.

Conversion from steam to diesel was delayed until 1963 for my father, so he had a goodly period sampling a very full range of Western steam locomotives. Meanwhile the footplatemen from other depots who surrounded us at Wharncliffe Gardens were undergoing their conversion training and not always enjoying it. Talk in the pub was of studying unfamiliar manuals, learning new terms and new techniques, but above all, they complained of the vibration and fumes which gave them headaches. A King's Cross driver of long standing committed suicide, but that was exceptional. The attachment of the men in their fifties to the older form of traction was very striking. The rough and ready training, the long years of back-breaking shovelling, the constant miasma of coal dust in which they worked, the violent jerking and rolling to which they were constantly subjected while on the move were all acceptable, understood parts of a man's life on the footplate. The advantages of sitting in a padded seat with a 'second-man' (as the fireman was renamed) to make a pot of tea on the thoughtfully provided stove, the cleaner clothes and hands were all discounted as if they hardly existed in the reckoning. In addition to all the changes there stalked the fear of redundancy. Diesels only really needed one man aboard, they were faster and needed less preparation by the engineman. Few seemed to like the change.

Preparations for express journeys started at home. Some time before going down to the sheds, driver Joby would produce the working timetable and in his neat copperplate handwriting, would transcribe the run into a pocket notebook that he would carry in his donkey jacket. Before an afternoon shift, lunch was at 12.30pm, plain, simple but tasty and substantial, usually with a large dab of Pan Yan pickle on the side of the plate. There was almost a ritual donning of overalls, donkey jacket and grease cap, then the invariable walk down to Warwick Avenue station on the Bakerloo line, for a tube train to Willesden Junction. Only on night shift, when there was a works train from Paddington, did this have to be changed. Old Oak Lane led from the Underground to the engine shed, past grimy LNWR terraces and the rival shed of Willesden Junction, always regarded as inferior, since it was largely concerned with goods traffic. A friendly nod to the gatekeeper took him into the depot and then on to the office where he signed on and read the notices, an impressive and comprehensive array that had to be inwardly digested along with the working timetable. Slacks, diversions, changes of mate or even of duty were notified here. A return trip to Bristol was diagrammed, with a Castle as motive power. The fireman was usually to be found in the canteen, so after picking him up and making sure that he had read the notices, they went into the roundhouse to find their engine. A check on tools, oil in the mechanical lubricator, then a thorough inspection was carried out to prevent problems later. With only a flare lamp for light, a pit inspection of the motion, noting any wear, metal shavings and looseness, was a pre-condition for a long journey. Any minor defects were booked, then, with boiler pressure rising as the fireman plied his shovel, the engine trundled on to the turntable and out into the yard. The inside motion and new controls of GWR engines were the things that took most getting used to after the outside valve gear and bucket seats of LNER engines, but my father appreciated the more thoughtful layout of Western engines.

Once in daylight, a further visual check was made to see that there were no leaky steam pipes, coal and water levels were looked at, as this was the last chance of doing anything about it. As the engine backed down the yard, a King from Bristol was coming in, so a few words were exchanged about conditions along the line. Late news supplemented the notice-board and unofficial points were often most valuable, especially on the whereabouts of inspectors. The yard signal gave right of way on the empty stock road to Paddington, under the massive retaining wall of the Grand Union Canal, up and over the main line tracks at Kensal Green, past the gasworks and on through the brick canyon to Royal Oak, where the engine paused at a signal until given right of way to back down on the Bristol express. All the while empty stock was moving in and out of Paddington behind fussy little pannier tank engines. Twenty years ago most trains were serviced at Old Oak, with none of the quick lick and a turnround of today. Locospotters under Bishop's Bridge on platform 10 busily noted down all the engines moving in and out, reserving a special glance for the polished giants on the expresses.

Driver Joby's mate, a reliable lad from South Wales, donned rubber gloves heavy with grease before jumping down between engine and carriages to couple engine and train, paying particular attention to the brake pipe. This was later visually checked both by driver and guard, who took no chances on so

77

vital a matter. The guard announced a load of 382tons behind the engine and warned that more time would be needed at Bath, where a lot of parcels had to be unloaded. He would appreciate a slightly early arrival.

My father's driving philosophy was a smooth run and arrival on time, so he took care to anticipate delays, obtained all the information available on likely delays so as to be able to act accordingly. Complete rapport between driver and mate meant that a good head of steam was constantly maintained. An incandescent fire of moderate thickness with a new layer of steam coal added every few minutes was my father's ideal in the long narrow firebox. He appreciated the much better quality of the coal at Old Oak, so much less sulphurous than the Nottingham-shire coal used at Neasden. A gentle start building up to a steady 70mph, a gentle easing well before known slacks followed by a gradual rather than spectacular recovery along the billiard table of a line to Swindon was the norm. A judicious balance between cut-off and regulator was nicely matched to the fireman's 'little and often' policy with the coal and water. Shrivenham was passed with half a minute in hand, so the time had come to ease the speed down before the Swindon stop. As the gradient was gently upwards, this could be done so that it was almost imperceptible to the passengers, resulting in a smooth arrival.

Drivers were always on their best behaviour when starting from Swindon, past the works that produced their engines, under the critical gaze of those at the heart of the system. The slight rise past the works soon gave way to a gentle down gradient where speed was gained for the rise into Chippenham. Thereafter it was downhill all the way from Corsham, the most exhilarating part being Box Tunnel. It was best to shut the regulator tight as the train propelled the engine down the 1 in 100 gradient that started at the tunnel mouth and continued well beyond it. That avoided the smoke and steam filling the cab to an uncomfortable extent, although if one passed an up goods train in the tunnel, pollution problems existed whatever measures were taken. A gradual opening of the regulator once daylight was reached resulted in steady acceleration to Bathford, where the approach to Bath Spa started. The remainder of the journey down the Avon Valley was through the crowded approaches to Bristol; tunnels, junctions and slacks precluding the measured stride of the rest of the journey, but the sweep into Temple Meads station was always welcome. Tea, a newspaper and a short rest from the absolute concentration was at hand. The reassuring automatic train control was a help, especially in bad weather, but it was the undivided attention of driver and mate that brought the train in safely day after day and it took its toll in nervous energy.

Plymouth, Wolverhampton, Cardiff and Oxford as well as the Bristol road were all learned under steam conditions. Those reflexes which allowed preventive action to be taken were conditioned by constant passage over hundreds of miles of first-class track on Castles, Kings and lesser engines, but towards the end of steam in 1963, my father was finally moved on to regular diesel work, mostly the diesel-hydraulics – Hymeks, Warships and Westerns. Increased speed led to the end of lodging turns, allowing a return trip to Exeter in the one shift rather than Paddington to Plymouth, a rest in the hostel and then return. Steam turns became fewer and fewer, but one further great run awaited my father. As the only ex-Great Central man at Old Oak he was given No 7029 *Clun Castle* on 27 March 1965 on an Ian Allan railtour of the Midlands. The engine was in its usual magnificent condition, a fitting climax to forty-one years on the footplate, although there were yet five more years of largely express work to come on diesels. Despite offers of early retirement with a cash sum, my father worked until his sixty-fifth birthday, bringing in a milk train from Weston-super-Mare on his very last run. Nearly half a century had been spent on the railways, spanning the period from the eve of amalgamation to the complete dieselisation of non-electrified lines on British Rail. For those who could pass the trials of the early years, it was indeed a job for life.

Neasden, King's Cross and Old Oak Common together with

Camden, Kentish Town and Nine Elms provided the glamour jobs for London drivers in steam days. Bath Road, Canton, Laira, Gateshead and Kingmoor were all names to conjure with when the giants of steam, human and metallic, were mentioned in the same breath as mileage payments and lodging turns. Yet all over the country there were hundreds of smaller sheds providing the motive power for branch lines, coal trains, dock complexes and cross-country lines. Staff numbers in such sheds were counted in dozens rather than hundreds, there was much less specialisation and probably more comradeship. Where everybody knew everybody else it was a case of fit in or get out. There was no room for separate facilities, little cabins for yard staff, others for different grades of shed and running staff. In the largest sheds a fireman dare not enter the drivers' room except to make a request or deliver a message. Moreover, in both environments benches were reserved by seniority and tradition, and woe betide an interloper. The life of a young fireman and his drivers at a minor shed on the East Coast main line brings out the contrasts between these differing kinds of shed.

Few who joined the railway service immediately after World War II could have dreamed that the way of life so familiar at that time would be dead within two decades. Ken Saunders left school at sixteen to join the LNER at Hitchin shed in 1946. Staff shortages meant that little time was spent on cleaning and other menial shed tasks before the novice found himself, shovel in hand on shunting jobs or pick-up goods runs. His acute attention to detail gives the flavour of those early footplate days in the last months of the LNER:

My first lessons in the art of observation took place as promotion into the 'outside yard link' provided me with daily runs to St Neots or to Royston. In that link we had mostly day work, signing on early in the morning. The 5.20am turn took us to St Neots, tender first on a J15, No 5479, taking with us from the down yard at Hitchin a short train of oddments for Sandy, Tempsford and St Neots. Rarely, one had a wagon for Barford Electricity Power Station, the long trains of coal for that cathedral like place being in the hands of New England men who worked those heavy trains southwards to Tempsford, ran round them and set off back to the long curving sidings which they had passed some 30 minutes or so earlier.

Even rarer there was an excursion into the connecting loop between the GN main line and the LNW line from Bedford to Cambridge about a mile north of Sandy. There a line of wagons would be picked up and drawn out, tyres protesting on tight curves and rusty rails, protesting it seemed at being disturbed from their long vigil on that line. For 20 minutes or so Sandy Junction signal-box, clinging precariously to the embankment on the up side would come alive; well-oiled levers would move rusty point blades over well-oiled chairs, and when the performance was completed the box would be locked up again, left to its own gently decaying devices and the shunter/signalman from Sandy would remount his equally decaying bicycle and set off back to his cabin for breakfast. We would trundle off northwards, the cab sometimes sheeted against the driving rain, passing the solitary hangar in a field near Everton signal-box scarcely remembering that only a few years before some of the bravest people involved in Hitler's war waited in that hangar at the dead of night to board the Lysanders which took them and dropped them over enemy occupied France.

Having uncoupled from our train at St Neots the first job was breakfast. We shared the porters room with Freddie, a corpulent man of mischievous features and habits. A never-ending sequence of practical jokes perpetrated on all and sundry filled the hours in between the comings and goings of the few stopping passenger trains at that station. He was also an expert and dedicated gardener and was as likely to be seen arched over his potatoes as he was to be stretched upwards to clean the station lights or signs. Eric, the shunter, lived in and was landlord of the pub in the station yard, a convenient arrangement for both himself and imbibing train crews. For several hours wagons were moved from here to there, and once daily we drew a line of them down the shunting spur at the north of the station, the back of the tender reaching out to come level with milepost 52, the furthest north point attained by men in the outside yard link.

Time was marked by the passage of main line trains thundering through the station or occasional glimpses of the buses on the road connecting St Neots with Cambridge. We listened half-heartedly to the coal merchants bemoaning the late arrival of wagons of coal so urgently needed for their customers' fireplaces and their profits, even promising to keep a look out for them. In season, sticks of rhubarb or heads of cauliflower were given space in the cab cupboards, we recompensing the donor with a half of the local beer bought for only

81

pennies from a smiling Eric over his shining counter. It was a leisurely turn, much enjoyed by the men in that link and it had a spectacular conclusion to each day's business.

The lunchtime procession of southbound expresses kept the up main line quite busy but there was a brief gap in this parade, just long enough for No 5479 to get a main line run all the way back to Hitchin. Shunting over, the signalman would enquire as to whether we were 'runners' or not and if the answer was 'yes' we would stand poised ready to leave the very moment the dolly signal turned its head.

With the tail end of a Leeds to King's Cross express barely out of sight under Barford Bridge, the points would change and Teddy Haig's hand would reach out for the regulator. 'Right mate' I would shout out as the appropriate wire tightened up so that by the time the actual miniature signal showed clear we were already moving forward in pursuit of the now out of sight train. The signalman shouted at us as we passed the box, always the same message day after day: 'Pullman's behind you at Huntingdon'. No 5479 would be gaining speed as the Tees Tyne Pullman was easing for the 70mph limit at Offord. A fast run to Hitchin could be achieved in 22 minutes, this providing just sufficient margin of time between the two expresses for a J15 to get home in one go. It was the highlight of the outside yard link so far as I was concerned. That little locomotive was a star performer indeed and when Teddy shut off steam for the brief descent from Langford Bridge to Arlesley, the clattering motions set up a noise like a thousand boilersmiths tapping away at a thousand firebox stays. Once through that station, Haig would open her up again, three-quarters regulator or so and the engine would nose forward towards home whilst the now nearly empty tender swayed from side to side. A spirited dash through Hitchin station concluded the show. Like as not the Pullman would dash by as we were setting back into the shed sidings, its crew whistling the derisory 'one long, one short' greeting if we had cut it fine: No 5479 would be left, handbrake on, under the coal chute and we would sign off about 1.35pm, 15 minutes overtime per day supplementing the already earned time and a quarter 'night rate' from 5.20am to 6.00am.

Sandy shunt allowed one an extra half an hour or so in bed and once the daily routine of signing on, preparing the engine had been completed we ran, light engine, to Sandy station and yard. In those days there was an interchange of wagons between the LNW line and the GN line and a miscellany of loads, mostly of agricultural or horticultural produce were shunted to and fro from their yard to ours. I say specifically, 'their yard' and 'our yard' for although we were all railwaymen together on a by now nationalised railway network we were still GN men to them and they were 'Wessie' men to us. Seldom indeed did we exchange more than a brief word, a cursory glance with a nod of the head being regarded as sufficient breach of the 'loyalty' barrier between us. Sandy yard was not large enough to keep us very busy and a fair amount of time was spent either watching the trains go by or watching the herons which nested in the pine trees on top of the hill to the east of the station. They swooped down to the tiny streams criss-crossing Sandy Heath on the west side of the line and often provided entertainment on the banks of these waters. Periodically a seemingly dormant heron would stab at the water and the wriggling tail or head of a fish or an eel would slither down its gullet. In the breeding season it would take off, scarcely clearing the roof of a passing train and make for its ungainly nest. At other times it would, once again, become quite stationary and apparently lifeless.

Biggleswade shunt was quite different. It meant signing on at 5.35am and taking the depot's only N2 tank engine out for the day. The closed-in cab was a godsend on a cold winter's morning but was far too hot for comfort in the summer. It also had a reversing screw and not a throw over lever, which, as the day wore on taxed the driver's arms. Often as not the young fireman in that link got his first 'driving turns' in on that locomotive, turns that ended abruptly when a complaining shunter drew the driver's attention to a string of wagons flying down the yard at considerable speed with the assistant shunter chasing after them. It was a curiously laid out yard with a diamond crossing right in the centre of it. For half an hour one would be shunting across the yard from south-east to north-west, then a change of tactics would lead to a north-east to south-west session during which the fireman had to be on constant look-out, translating the hand signals from the shunter to audible signals to the driver. A further inconvenience was that the fireman was on the side away from the main line and had to peer over the driver's shoulder to watch the Capitals Limited or the Scotsman fly by at 10.20am or 10.50am or thereabouts.

The seasons, as they followed each other, provided one with intimate study of the smallholder and his land, for Biggleswade was a busy place. By midday a number of wagons were partly loaded with vegetables destined for Covent Garden, onions sharing a 12 tonner with carrots whilst potatoes required several wagons for themselves alone. Sprouts alternated with cabbage or cauliflowers, according to season, as did celery and tomatoes. The compensation for an otherwise dreary turn of duty was to stock up with vegetables during that week. Most of this produce was legally acquired but there were, from time to time, ingenious ways of supplementing one's purchases. One driver used regularly to tie the sleeve ends of his railway issued raincoat with string and then fill the sleeves with onions or carrots or small cauliflowers. Tomatoes, filched from a wagon in the yard, were carefully packed into sandwich tins whilst a stick of celery, with a string looped around it would be secured from prying eyes underneath one's overall trousers and dangled from either belt or braces. A decent sized handkerchief would hold and hide a breakfast of mushrooms, one driver specialising in the art of stuffing them inside the rim of his shiny-top cap. Freddie . . . was unbeatable for he had a place for just about everything there was available. His wife once said that watching him unload the day's ill-gotten gains was like watching a magician producing rabbits out of thin air. Had he ever claimed to be carrying swedes or turnips in his armpits nobody would have thought of denying the claim. At 5.30am he was a thin wispy little man, but perched precariously on his unbraked bicycle at going home time he was clearly overweight. A magnificent tale, related many times to an admiring audience, told how he was walking away from the engine shed one lunchtime, laden to the gills with veg of one sort and another and carrying a 14lb sack of onions when he met Tom, the railway policeman.

'Hallo Fred, what you got there?'

'A bag of onions. I brought the bloody things with me this morning for Alf . . . and the rotten bugger had the day off so I'm taking them home again.'

'How much are you selling them for mate?'

'Two shillings.'

'I'll have 'em if you like.'

A florin changed hands as did the bag of onions and Tom, with an appreciative sniff at the bag, set off on his way. Freddie went his way too, doubtless investing the two bob in the liquid delights of the Woolpack pub.

The following morning when Freddie signed on duty there was a note for him from Tom. It said: 'Saw Alfy . . . last night and told him about the onions. He says he doesn't mind waiting till you're on the Biggleswade job again in six weeks time.

cheers.

PS. I'm on holiday that week and my relief is hotter than the onions. Tom.'

As far as I recall Alf didn't get his onions, that is assuming he didn't take delivery in small pocketsized batches.

Another turn in the link brought us into close contact with the civil engineering department of the railway. Hitchin boasted a large

A group of Stratford-upon-Avon & Midland Junction Railway officers. From left to right: G.H. Payton (bank manager); A.E. Diggins (secretary and traffic manager); W.M. Bell (Parliamentary agent); Russell Willmott (engineer and locomotive superintendent); S. Herbert (deputy chairman); C.S.M. Bayes (solicitor); Harry Willmott (chairman); and T.H. Crampton (former chairman, East & West Junction Railway) (*Locomotive & General Railway Photographs*)

Managers sixty years on: a group at Liverpool Street station in 1950, including Dick Hardy holding the smokebox handrail and Gerard Fiennes second from right (*British Rail*)

Railwaymen at war: LNER B12 No 8488 crosses the temporary bridge at Grove Road after VI attack in June 1944 (*National Railway Museum*)

King's Cross engine shed, Great Northern Railway (*Locomotive & General Railway Photographs*)

engineers depot and one of our turns was 6.30am engineers pilot No 2. (No 1 pilot was a higher link turn and they took train loads of materials out daily in preparation for future and mainly weekend relaying, repair works.) It was a certainty that No 2 pilot locomotive was the worst available one from the shed. Often a D3 or D2, probably No 2148 or 2163, occasionally an Atlantic, No 2822 or 2828, sometimes a 'foreigner' (a locomotive borrowed by Hitchin loco depot after it had strayed into the area). Foreigners that I recall include a Hornsey J50 No 8946, on its way to Doncaster for a badly needed and long overdue shopping. Hatfield N1s or N2s, a Colwick J39 with a steam reverser that only worked into forward gear. We even had class K1/1 No 1997 *MacCailin Mor* for a day in the then black BR livery and a long way from its home on the West Highland line. From the same area we acquired, for several days, a K2, probably No 1739. A C12 from Grantham depot turned up on one occasion and I spent a hard day supplementing near non-existent vacuum brakes by continually winding the handbrake on or off.

The yard itself was a curious place, the sidings having been laid to whim and fancy rather to any distinguishable pattern. Odd short stretches of line appeared periodically in the most unlikely places, the rail itself being worn out, lightweight lengths laid to indeterminate gauge and to impossible curves. The heavier locomotives squealed a protest as they navigated these sidings and not infrequently came off the road. In this situation the 'resident' shunter/guard – I say 'resident' since they never seemed to go home – would whistle up for the enormous steam crane stationed in the south-eastern corner of that yard and it would trundle along and lift the locomotive back on the rails within minutes. Work would continue as if derailments were a necessary part of the job.

The south-eastern corner of the yard was a fascinating area for here vast and complicated crossovers and points were prefabricated, checked, altered, checked again and then dismantled and finally loaded on to wagons ready for despatch to wherever it was to be installed. This prefabrication process was quite extraordinary for no one ever seemed to have a drawing. A large area was cleared, odd sleepers laid out to mark the extremities of the layout to be con-structed and gradually the intervening space was filled with sleepers, crossing timbers, chairs, rails and check rails. Then a marvellous character would appear to check the work. He was an inspector employed, not by the railway but by a sub-contracting company and he wielded immense power over a large gang of even larger Irish navvies. A relic of an earlier era to be sure. He cursed them from dawn to dusk, they retaliated in like manner and together they installed in record times intricate networks of rails at King's Cross station, or at Ferme Park, or Hitchin or anywhere else in the King's Cross area. Summer or winter he always wore a silk scarf knotted round his neck, the trailing ends of which, went under his armpits and were knotted again at the back. His nodding head and sharply peaked black cap cut through the air like a scythe and his dislike for engines and engine crews was vehement. They wore his rails out and that was unforgivable. It was said that he invariably got slightly drunk before he started on a job and worked himself towards sobriety as the day or night wore on. A measure of respect was accorded to him since he was reputed to know the names, birthdays, even the antecedents of every publican within walking distance of the lineside between King's Cross and Peterborough, including the then many branch lines. He could charm beer out of a pub at 4.00pm or 4.00am and distributed bottles of Guinness, sparingly, to everyone connected with the relaying operation except the engine crews.

He finally disappeared from the railway scene about the time of the Potters Bar Tunnel dualling scheme and the GN line was the poorer for his departure into retirement.

One of the comparatively permanent sidings in the engineer's yard was known as the middle road. It was long and straight holding about 50 to 60 wagons. There were no buffer stops at the end of this north facing line, only a very steep bank leading up to the lane crossing Hitchin South bridge. One of the 'party pieces' when pushing wagons into this siding was to pretend not to see the frantic hand signals given from a variety of places by one Fred Odell, and watch as the end wagon started climbing up this bank. One had to be a little careful, for if the wagon got too far up this one in two gradient its buffers would get locked under the buffers of the wagon to which it was hooked. Fred could be spotted, high up on a pile of sleepers, or hanging precariously from a telegraph pole, even astride the ridge of a shed roof. He would be gesticulating wildly and we would draw the line of wagons back again slowly. If the end wagon's buffers had got locked, the furthermost end of the end wagon but one would rise into the air, it would become a two-wheeler and would remain in this precarious posture until the crane came and restored the situation to normal. Fred always got his own back, a handful of salt in our kettle being the favourite retribution though on one occasion he relieved himself in the cab of a J3, No 4122 the stench being quite awful for several hours, during which many gallons of boiling water scoured the sodden floorboards.

The yard was home depot for a string of former GNR six wheeled coaches, no longer finished in teak but in black and with DE

(Departmental Engineer) numbers. On jobs where large numbers of
the platelaying crews were involved, four or five of these would set off
from the yard behind an ex-GNR 0-6-0 or an Atlantic and the sight of
this 'period' train climbing away towards Stevenage was pure
nostalgia. Sometimes a broken rail out in the country necessitated our
taking a repair train out to the place and somewhat unlikely
concoctions presented the casual observer with a contrast to the more
usual trains. An N2 would pass through the various stations on the
main line with a 60ft long rail wagon and a steam crane between two
GNR six-wheeled carriages, more smoke coming from the crane than
from the loco. On a warm day sunbathing bodies were strewn over the
rail wagons, sharing its hard floor with a single length of rail and the
cutting gear. Perhaps it would be a class C12 or D3 with two GNR
carriages, one either end of a wagon loaded with a set of replacement
points, two cranes, one steam and one hand operated, making up this
unlikely load. When these jobs occurred the footplate crew invariably
received from Fred Odell explicit instructions that if any pheasants or
partridges were spotted lying between the rails (having been knocked
down by a passing train), they were to stop. He would retrieve it and
later a pack of cards would be cut to determine whose table would be
graced by the luckless bird. He also provided the pack of cards and
nearly always won the cut. I spotted a decimated crow just north of
Tempsford on one such journey and the driver stopped the train,
gesticulating to Fred as to the bird's whereabouts. He nipped off
across the lines and we set off as quietly as possible leaving him with
the better part of a half-mile to cover to re-entrain, this time without a
bird. Since Fred was my uncle and the crime of 'assault on the person'
carried no weight within a family, I received a smart and smarting
kick up the backside when the opportunity for such undignified
behaviour arose.

Of such pleasant memories were Ken Saunders' early years on
the footplate made. After he had convinced the locomotive
inspector of his ability to handle a B1 on the Cambridge run,
promotion and transfer to King's Cross was followed by
extensive main-line firing and further promotion to driver at the
incredibly early age of twenty-four. For the next six years a life of
pure magic based at Top Shed followed, driving Pacifics and
their smaller brethren up and down the East Coast main line with
a verve that can still be appreciated when he takes the regulator
on the North York Moors Railway or bombs around Brands

# 6
# *The Guv'nors*

Every disciplined organisation needs officers to control the men. The early managerial class in railway service was often recruited from army and naval officers whose ideas on uniform, smartness, timing and harsh discipline were readily observable in practice. So close was the parallel in the early years of the GWR that a correspondent wrote to the management seriously suggesting that trains should be run like ships with a train captain, cosily ensconced in an iron and glass cabin on the tender, to oversee the progress of the train from his 'bridge', just like a naval captain.

The man entrusted with the management of the greatest railway amalgamation of the nineteenth century, which brought the London & North Western Railway into being in 1846 was Capt Mark Huish, a soldier who had served the East India Company in Bengal until his appointment in 1837 at the age of twenty-nine as secretary to the Glasgow, Paisley & Greenock Railway. This was followed by the general managership of the much larger Grand Junction Railway in 1841, which was to be a key constituent of the vast new company, the largest commercial operation of its day and destined to remain one of the three largest railway companies until 1923.

The growth of a management system that was both effective and efficient owes much to Huish and his contemporaries. The creation of railway settlements, well provided with substantial cottages and good amenities, was seen as the basis of a loyal and contented staff, while a clear chain of command through executive officers was one way of relieving the directors of day-to-day decisions on every subject from staff to pollution. The model emerged by the 1850s of a pyramid of power with professional managers and directors heading committees which took major decisions, while leaving day-to-day running to their well-briefed subordinates.

Joseph Tatlow, who later became a general manager of two Irish railways, remembered the superiors in his early days in the 1860s:

> The office to which I was assigned had about thirty clerks, all of whom, except the chief clerk, occupied tall stools at high desks. I was one of the two assistants to a senior clerk. The senior was middle-aged and passing rich on £80 a year. A quiet, steady, respectable married man, well-dressed, cheerful, contented, he had by care and economy, out of his modest salary, built for himself a snug little double-breasted villa, in a pleasant outskirt of the town, where he spent his spare hours in his garden and enjoyed a comfortable and happy life.
>
> Except the chief clerk whose salary was about £160, I do not believe there was another whose pay exceeded £100 a year. The real head of the office, or department as it was called, was not the chief clerk but one who was ranked higher still and was styled Head of Department, and who received a salary of £300.

Differentials even at this level were of an order that did not survive long in the following century.

Continued railway expansion meant that there were plenty of opportunities for promotion even later in the nineteenth century. Within fifteen years of being assistant to a senior clerk at Derby, Joseph Tatlow had risen up the promotion ladder via a post in Scotland to be general manager of the newly amalgamated Belfast & County Down Railway where he found that 'the condition of the permanent way, the rolling stock, and the stations was anything but good, and as the traffic showed capacity for development, to stint expenditure would have been but folly. I do not think, however, the outlay would have been so liberal as it was but for Lord Pirrie, who was an active and influential director, though there were also on the board several other business men of energy and position.' The importance of a good working relationship between manager and board was highlighted at about that time on the other side of the country on the Great Eastern Railway where Charles Parkes (of Parkeston

Quay fame) worked with Lord Claud Hamilton to take that railway into an age of profitable expansion during a depression.

On the Belfast & County Down, Tatlow found that it was the . . .

> rolling stock that demanded the most urgent attention – engines, carriages and wagons and especially carriages. Of carriages there were not enough for the traffic of the line, and many were in a very sorry condition, particularly those taken over from the Holywood & Bangor Railway. One weekend, soon after I joined the service, I had all the passenger carriages brought into Belfast, except those employed in running Sunday trains, and early on the Sunday morning with the company's locomotive and mechanical engineer I examined each carriage thoroughly from top to bottom, inside and out, above and below, and with his practical help and expert knowledge, noted carefully down the defects of each. He worked with a will, delighted that someone as enthusiastic and even younger than himself was now in charge. He little suspected, I am sure, how ignorant I was of practical matters, as I kept my own counsel which was my habit when prudence so dictated.

The later traffic apprentice scheme of the NER and later LNER eliminated the mechanically unversed manager, but the sheer range of the tasks was made the more daunting.

The detailed report to the board and the prospect of more traffic won the day, so Tatlow got his carriages and within three years his former chief at Derby, Sir James Allport, inspected the little Ulster railway, approving of the 5½ per cent dividend and the improved service with reduced rates that the management shake-up seems to have produced.

There was another side to management: that of discipline. The rules were harsh, but their successful application demanded flexibility, otherwise there would certainly have been no work-force, so easy was it to be dismissed. Tatlow's assistant 'discovered that the man in charge of the cloakroom was guilty of peculation, had been tampering with the tickets, and appropriating small sums. I sent for him, talked to him very severely, sent him home, and told him that he should hear what would be done. An hour later, I heard he was dead; that on his way home he had purchased a bottle of laudanum and swallowed the contents.' Few reacted so badly, others were handed over to the courts for punishment.

General managers were the key figures in the salaried hierarchy, far more important than the engineers in precedence and salary terms, despite the emphasis on the latter in mechanical histories. After moving to Dublin, Joseph Tatlow became one of the three most important managers in Ireland, sat on a Royal Commission and was eventually made a director of the Midland Great Western Railway in 1917. He came to love Ireland deeply, remaining in Dalkey, just south of Dublin during the Troubles, which coincided with his retirement. The complete identification with the organisation and willingness to work through a problem to conclusion became a mark of the most successful railway management. A head containing encyclopaedic knowledge, an ability to think on one's feet, to handle people from directors to lad porters with tact and sympathy, sound engineering knowledge and administrative ability, were but the most important qualifications for the job of general manager. Not all those appointed succeeded at the job, but those who did, like Sir Henry Oakley on the Great Northern or Sir Herbert Walker on the London & South Western, were instrumental in making their railways run extremely well.

The 'office boy to general manager' story was not a figment of Victorian literary imagination. There were many cases of it and the publicity that they received from popular writers of the period served as a spur to poor but ambitious lads to join the railways as a means of getting on in life. There were other ladders within the railways as well. Office life does not appeal to everyone; indeed to many railwaymen, the most romantic and rewarding part of railway work was amid the smoke, grease and cinders of the operating side, where the route to the top was via the all-important role of shedmaster. Beyond this lay motive power superintendent, works manager and chief mechanical or electrical engineer. But, as always, one first had to learn the nuts and bolts of the job from the basics upwards.

The main route for those who wished to become top men on the engineering side was by apprenticeship. The existing engineers were generally permitted to take pupils for a premium, which was added to their already substantial salaries. Most apprenticeships were served at the great works and the able pupil came to the notice of the great man, who would recommend him to others at the end of his time or even take him on to his own staff. A whole host of posts were in the gift of the chief engineers, so a clean record, diligence and willingness were important to promotion prospects. Some apprenticeships were served on the running side at depots such as Willesden and even remote Woodford Halse. They had the advantage of not requiring a premium, but the chance of catching the eye of those responsible for important appointments was less.

David William (Bill) Harvey was one of the first generation of LNER apprentices. His education at Whitgift School, Croydon, was well ahead of that of earlier days, but the Latin and French were of little help in Doncaster works in the early 1920s. The apprenticeship under the aegis of the formidable Sir Nigel Gresley was rigorous, but all the essentials for a mechanical career were covered, and included such high points as the erection of *Flying Scotsman*, an engine with which Bill has remained intimately associated.

Once out of his time at Doncaster, Bill was sent to Neasden, where my father had started his railway career nearly five years before. In 1927, Neasden was still a very smart, clean and tidy depot. The shed walls were whitewashed down to shoulder height and tarred below that. All the pits in the machine shop were whitewashed, the engines and floors were models of cleanliness. Especially important was the lack of ash lying about. Under the command of Mathew Robinson, son of the former chief mechanical engineer J. G. Robinson, the old Great Central line was still a proud railway. The A5s and Directors were immaculately turned out for their work of running the important outer suburban and express traffic.

Bill's first job at Neasden was on a Director, *Walter Burgh*

*Gair*, which needed work done on its bogie wheels, necessitating use of the drop table. He worked with an old fitter of uncertain age, Jimmy Simmonds, who was still there when Bill returned as shedmaster in 1949. He instructed the newcomer in the everyday problems of shed maintenance, so different from the Doncaster plant where there were facilities to tackle almost anything. One of the boilersmiths, Jack Brown, was an old LNWR man who had clashed with the redoubtable Francis Webb by suggesting that the water-tube grate on some of Webb's boilers would not work since convection currents rise. After this incident he was shunned at Crewe as being a dangerous individual, so it was probably with relief on both sides that he came south with the greatly expanded Great Central line. Under such men the young passed apprentice learned the craft of making a silk purse out of a sow's ear by dint of ingenuity and common sense. The provision of adequate motive power in serviceable condition is not just a rule by which shedmasters and budding shedmasters live; it is the canon that overshadows all else and is often difficult to fulfil, but is somehow usually managed.

The next move was to Top Shed at King's Cross, built many decades before Neasden in yellow brick, long since begrimed. It was the premier depot of the old Great Northern Railway, very congested, but clean and tidy apart from the external brickwork. The morale was generally high except among newly drafted footplatemen, but some of its equipment was in the museum-piece category even in 1929. The beam engine driving the shafting in the workshop was purchased for £365 when the depot was built in the 1860s. It was of the Watt type and was at least second-hand even then. It was housed in a small building next to the boiler house and was shown to the newcomers, who noticed that its flywheel had wooden teeth made of applewood. The workshop was lit by a large gas lamp with four mantles which used a whitewashed board 10ft in diameter as a reflector. The shop was very wet inside and large chunks of plaster were missing, but for young fellows, the joy of life overcame such inconveniences. When the foreman could be relied on to be away for a period, they had a favourite game of playing hoop-la with piston rings, using engine buffers as targets.

Footplate experience was essential for a trainee, so that he could appreciate the machines and the nature of the work that would eventually come under his control. Suburban trains to Alexandra Palace and Hertford on the footplate of an N2 were pleasurable experiences, but feelings about the trip down the 'Hole' to Moorgate were mixed. When the engine left York Road the condenser valve was pulled over, so that exhaust steam was condensed by passing it through the side tanks. By Farringdon the water in the tanks was warm, by Aldersgate it was bubbling out of the vents, filling the cab with a dense white pall. It was similar to working in a Turkish bath. By Moorgate the water had to be discharged into a pit and the tanks refilled with cold water. The return was even worse, as the gradient was against the engine, culminating in a vicious 1 in 37 gradient on the hotel curve under the Great Northern Hotel. As the engine burst out of the tunnel, the crew leaned out of the cab to draw in lungfuls of 'King's Cross ozone', a curious combination of acetylene, engine smoke and steam, fish vapours, carbon monoxide and perhaps a little oxygen lurking somewhere – at least it was better than the atmosphere in the cab. But despite all the tunnel work from Moorgate to Finsbury Park, the engines were kept very clean.

The next move was to Stratford in 1934, then under the command of Leslie Parker who put passed apprentices through their paces. For those who survived, he was thought to be an excellent guv'nor. He tried his young men beyond their capacities, knowing what was ahead of them when they were given their own commands. Working for him was like being in a gym all the time, but to pass the grade there was to know that nothing much worse lay ahead. Brentwood depot was a sub-depot of Stratford, which in 1934 served as a turnround point for outer suburban traffic. It had been under a driver-in-charge, but Bill Harvey, as a young chargeman, was given the command as traffic grew after the widening of the lines to Shenfield.

Electrification was still over a decade away, so the nippy schedules had to be maintained by steam engines, not all of them too sprightly.

Brentwood was a lesson in man-management. One of the most trying characters was a passed cleaner nicknamed 'Master Panshine'. He lit up the engines required for early duty and called the men on to duty. An old Great Eastern driver, Arthur Ellingford, was particularly proud of his engine; indeed his Claud Hamilton 4-4-0 was the pride of the shed. Claud No 8791 was due to take out the 4.35am for Southend. Arthur arrived as usual in his spotless overalls and polished boots to find 30lb of steam on the dial and a firebox that was black inside, the coal piled up to the brick arch. The cleaner had slept in the messroom while the engine had cooked its overload of coal in the same way as a gas retort, resulting in coke in the cab, whose roof had been set afire, and tar oozing out of the tubes into the smokebox. The engine had to be retubed before further service, while the Romford pilot engine had to deputise on the Southend train.

The LNER tried to break down the exclusiveness of the old railway systems by transferring locomotives between areas. A class that was brought to Brentwood was the N2 from Scotland. Half-a-dozen of them shared the shed with the sole Claud. The drivers heartily disliked the engines and did all they could to fail them. They were the older engines in the class and had been badly used, their superheater elements had trouble with their joints and previous repairs appeared to have been carried out with hammers. Most of all, the men objected to the face-plate injectors, not at all like the Great Eastern injectors that they were used to. The worst of the bunch was No 4737, a wretched engine that leaked in every element 'like fountains in Trafalgar Square'. To put the matter right, Bill had to spend eight hours on the engine, softening the copper jackets to the elements over the messroom fire. No less than twenty-nine engines were used by Brentwood against the official allocation of six before matters were put to rights. It was a gruelling introduction to command, but promotion to Gorton followed. No union hours or conditions now – one was there until the job was done.

The training of potential managers in the twentieth century was little more scientific than in Tatlow's time. The North Eastern Railway pioneered the Traffic Apprentice Scheme, later taken up and widened by the LNER, which incorporated with it elements of Great Eastern practice, and in its final form was inherited by the nationalised railway system in 1948. Raw graduates and sometimes other promising management material were recruited and given a grounding in how the railways were run, learning most of the jobs that railwaymen did by being rapidly rotated through practical work experience in many parts of the system. A few months in a signal-box ended with the young man being put through his paces by a signalling inspector. With his back to the frame he would have to be able to go through the levers required for a number of complex movements, recognise audible signals and answer questions on emergency procedures before moving on to shunting in a large goods yard, acting as guard on an unbraked goods train, station porter, locomotive fireman and booking clerk. Through close contact, he learned in intimate detail how and how not to run a railway.

By his mid-twenties a traffic apprentice could take off his jacket and substitute for any of a multitude of railway jobs in an emergency. He spoke the same language as the men, could use all their specialised terms and attract their respect by being able to do their job and many others as well. It was a rough and ready training, far removed from the graduate business schools of the present day, but it gave the railways the managers who coped with the succession of crises that have enveloped the railways in the last five decades. Depression, war, nationalisation, loss of staple traffic and modernisation have all been coped with, yet the system that remains provides as good a service as any in Europe at its best and one that is much better than that provided in North America.

The traffic apprentice grew accustomed to long hours, frequent moves and problems of infinite variety requiring instant solutions, aimed at him the moment after they arose. Exposure to the critical eyes of those teaching and examining him in all the jobs that he performed meant that he was known throughout the system long before he was given his first permanent appointment. His faults and weaknesses would be discussed and analysed in messroom and platelayers' cabin alike. It was a gruelling yet highly selective introduction to railway work, demanding great physical and mental fitness. Those who survived knew that they could do the job.

Whereas in Victorian times the managers and engineers had been some of the best-paid men on the railways and indeed in the country, their relative position slipped alarmingly from World War I onwards. While the locomotive superintendent of the Great Eastern Railway in the 1880s was paid, with premiums from apprentices and earnings from patents, some £2,000 per annum, or some twenty-five times the pay of an average railwayman, his successors in the 1930s had a much more difficult job to do for little more. Their team of assistants, shedmasters and others were paid proportionately far less and promotion was slow with the retrenchment of the railways in the face of competition, amalgamation and depression. Not surprisingly, some of the more active young men sought experience and authority overseas.

After Gorton, Bill Harvey did a tour of duty in Nigeria, where railway life was truly in the raw and help of the kind available from Stratford or Doncaster was thousands of miles away. It was a formative period, giving him a good grounding for the different but equally trying war years that followed his return to England in the spring of 1940. The old Great Central and Great Northern lines and their problems occupied him more than fully for the next decade, with postings as far apart as Neasden and Nottingham.

The problems of the 1930s for middle managers had been largely those of trying to run an excellent service with inadequate funds. The searchlight of publicity had played strongly on streamlined expresses and luxury trains, but ageing equipment, permanent way and penny-pinching all round had been the reality for those running the show. However, staffing and cleanliness had never been problems, while traditional discipline had been maintained. Wartime problems of maintenance and staffing were thought to be temporary. Once the boys came back, it was hoped that things would revert to their familiar pattern, but many did not return to their former jobs. Offers of easier and more remunerative work elsewhere took more men away from the railways than death and injury ever did. Thus shedmasters and other railway managers in the big cities had to cope with mounting problems when peace returned.

The contrast between urban and rural areas was extreme in the first decade after the war. Woodford Halse could keep engines in good repair, even clean them and readily obtain an adequate labour supply, whereas Old Oak Common was reduced to getting in clerks on a weekend basis to clean its engines. They badly needed the money, so an arrangement was made. Neglected, elderly engines and carriages were a poor advertisement for the newly nationalised industry, so standard locomotives and carriages had easy and accessible maintenance built into them.

Temporary wartime appointments of women to do all but the heaviest work on shed caused a revolution at the time. Tube cleaning, ash removal, cleaning and canteen work alike fell to them. Since in the aftermath of the war many men did not return, some women stayed on. Separate toilets and rest rooms were set aside for them. Some of the more militant made the rules as far as their treatment by management was concerned.

Other problems arose with time enforcement: a five-minute allowance before clocking-off time was usual in the mucky shed conditions of post-war King's Cross. Routine checking of the fair sex's whereabouts some 20 minutes before the end of work revealed no sign of them, apart from noises from their washroom. Warnings were issued to no avail, so suspension followed. At this point the shop steward intervened to defend what would have been regarded as a cause for dismissal in earlier days. Labour was too scarce to dismiss wholesale in 1945, so reinstatement followed, but with no formal agreement. It was the start of a downhill slide in some parts of the railway system that reached its nadir for Bill Harvey at Neasden in 1949. In the autumn of that year the 5.45pm train for High Wycombe failed with Barrington Ward, a leading member of the Railway Executive, aboard. Only a few old timers were left amongst the maintenance staff at Neasden, so when even the key train could not be relied on, action was called for and Bill Harvey was summoned from Norwich to restore the depot to some semblance of reliability.

Half of the locomotive allocation was awaiting repair so he called for eight fitters and started a programme to reduce this to 10 per cent. It was the hardest six months of his life but he succeeded. It was an uphill task all the time in a situation where a driver earned under £5 a week while a lad hardly out of school could make more doing a milk round with none of the dirt and depression that surrounded a London locomotive depot. Fortunately Neasden in 1949 *was* the nadir. The trains did keep running, if erratically at times, with the help of country depots and the efforts of the core of staff from happier days. In depots away from London, matters were considerably better.

Norwich in the early 1950s underwent its most massive change of main line motive power since the early years of this century. The introduction of the Britannias on the Great Eastern main line revolutionised train running, making the line the fastest and most reliable in the country. Norwich shed and workshops was an amalgam of ancient and modern. The main building dated from Norfolk Railway days, still retaining fireplaces in the walls to disperse the dangerous coke fumes of the early engines. The shed itself could take but a small proportion of the allocation, so that many locomotives spent much of their time in the open or in sub-sheds on the branch lines around Norfolk. The engines ranged in age from elderly J15s dating from the 1880s to the new Britannia class, although the majority of the allocation had been built before 1923. The workload was very varied, from main line expresses to pick-up goods trains, yet Norwich soon acquired an

Shelton Colliery Sidings signal-box and the North Staffordshire Railway signalman. The colliery was connected to the NSR by a branch from Hanley Junction on the Loop line (*Locomotive & General Railway Photographs*)

Interior of a standard Great Western Railway signal-box (*Locomotive & General Railway Photographs*)

Ken Saunders (centre) in the locomotive canteen at King's Cross after a record run

Cleaners at Neasden with an immaculate Great Central Railway Director 4–4–0 No 437 *Prince George* (*H.C. Casserley*)

enviable reputation for turnout, speed and availability. Attention to detail, a knack for doing things right first time and good human relations, together with endless hours of duty, combined to put the Norwich division on a very firm footing. There were always new developments that required further effort, retraining and redeployment of men. Diesel railcars arrived late in 1955, requiring new workshop accommodation. When they were put on the Wells line, they had to bring back boxes of whelks, which dripped corrosive slime from the luggage compartment into the running parts. Bill designed a zinc-lined waterproof tray for this traffic. Main line diesels from 1957 onwards required Norwich shed to be run as a mixed steam/diesel depot for the next five years, making great demands on engineering skills as well as space. Then the closure of the M&GN in 1959 brought about a massive redeployment of men and traffic that strained resources to the utmost.

Bill established a standard of express running by 1953 on the Liverpool Street to Norwich line that was not bettered until some twenty years later. Two hours became the standard and although this is now slightly improved according to the timetable, it rarely is in practice. The great concrete coaling stage that once dominated the shed has now been felled, the turntable has gone, the steam workshop now services diesels, but there was one return to steam when the V2 2-6-2 *Green Arrow* was brought back to its pristine condition in Norwich, ready for the opening of the National Railway Museum. *Duchess of Sutherland* and *Thundersley* at Bressingham near Diss, and the North Norfolk Railway's J15 at Sheringham have all benefited from Bill's skilled repairs in their Norfolk retirement. Despite his very successful introduction of diesels to Norfolk, where steam ceased as early as the spring of 1962, he is still a man of steam at heart, whose enthusiasm for his chosen career is unabated.

*Flying Scotsman* has been one of Bill's main concerns in the last ten years. He accompanied the engine on its tour of America and has done much to keep it running since its return to England. A stickler for having things done right, he works on a job as long as it takes, which can be all night and much of the next day in some cases. The other very important thing is that he carries those helping him all the way. Enthusiasm from the top is infectious. When one looks at the performances of Britannias in Coronation year, or at locomotives nearly a century old still working trains for enthusiasts, one should remember the guiding hand behind such achievements. A guv'nor motivates as well as commands.

Railway management comprised a hardy group of men. Those at the sharp end regularly expected to work six days a week or more for pay which in the early post-war days was only twice that of their employees. Cecil J. Allen whose job it was to check rails worth millions of pounds for the GER and then the LNER, had a salary which did not rise between 1917 and his retirement in 1946, yet the scope of the job increased and the cost of living exploded in the war years. The job of the guv'nor can only be described as a vocation, as the many autobiographies testify. Certainly in this century, nobody was in it for the money.

# 7
# *Railwaymen at War*

In both the world wars the railways played the major role in transport in Britain, their employees were tested to the full and not found wanting. Huge increases in traffic, government control, enrolment of many of the men in the forces and a large intake of women employees, all brought significant changes to operations, and in the aftermath of each war there were improvements in hours, working conditions and wages for the staff.

In World War I the main battle areas for British and later American forces, were in France, not far from the Channel ports. The requirements in men and materials were enormous and only the railways could move them to the ports and on to the steamers for France. British railwaymen flocked to the flag and were often released in the early days regardless of traffic needs. As an example, over a third of the LNWR staff, or 37,742 men, served with the colours. Of these over 4,000 were volunteers. The railways equipped and staffed the Railway Operating Division and its workshops in France and the Middle East, while coping with greatly increased traffic at home. The major works maintained their locomotive stocks to a lower standard than usual: repairs as and when necessary, simpler liveries, a dab and a patch when once repainting and overhaul would have been normal. Fewer new engines were built, older ones were kept in service. It was the same with structures, carriages and wagons the last two of which were raided to provide stock for government operations at home and overseas.

Older men stayed on past retirement, boys were tempted to start work as early as twelve years of age yet still the cry was for more labour, while the forces were demanding the release of more grades of men for armed service; so it came about that women were increasingly recruited to release men. They took on a wider and wider range of jobs, munitions work, cleaning, ticket collecting, clerical work and much else. As more and more space in the works was devoted to government contracts, so the proportion of girls in them increased. Portering and light engineering came their way, as did praise from the LNWR's war historian G.R.S. Darroch who wrote that 'they were not only amenable to reason and discipline, but became regular enthusiasts in the work on which they were engaged. Idling and indifference were qualities unknown, patience and perseverence became personified, and thanks to a highly efficient and praiseworthy organisation, coupled with a system of three consecutive eight hour shifts, the output of fuses rapidly rose from a mere 150 per week to as many as 4,000.' Despite their obvious success, women were rapidly despatched back to the kitchen sink in 1919 to release jobs for the demobilised menfolk.

Overtime became the norm for the railwaymen who did not change uniforms. Endless hours on footplate, in guard's van or signal-box recalled the excessive working hours of the Victorian years which had only recently been reduced by a combination of union agreements and legislation in the wake of accidents caused by the errors of overtired railwaymen. Zeppelin raids over London and the east coast added a new and scary dimension to the hazards of work. Occasional bombardment from the sea, as at Yarmouth and Hartlepool, generated a sense of danger fuelled by rumour, and prompted the creation of the sinister armoured train that patrolled lines along the Norfolk coast. Material damage was slight: a couple of bombs on Liverpool Street and another on St Pancras, while Derby works sustained damage from a Zeppelin in 1916 which was soon cleared up. All this was minor in comparison with what was happening in the trenches a mere hundred miles from London.

World War II was altogether more hazardous for those operating the home railways. Air power had greatly increased in range and striking power. After the invasion of France parts of the south coast were within shelling distance, while nowhere in the rest of the country was entirely secure and the railways were very important targets. On the other hand preparations were better this time. Control staffs were evacuated to country areas; for example, the Southern Railway was masterminded from Deepdene near Dorking and the old Great Central lines were supervised from Beaconsfield in Buckinghamshire. There was less danger that the system would start to resemble a headless chicken. It was at the individual level that the most vivid experiences were seen, heard and felt. The East End of London with its docks, factories and dense population was a prime target. The railwaymen who worked there through blitz and rocket attack were in the front line daily for months at a time.

Devonshire Street, Mile End, was one of those East End goods yards known to few but vitally important to the district as a distribution centre of coal and general goods. It was conceived in the days when horse and cart could only serve a two-mile radius from the goods yard, which is why the railways had so many dotted around London and other cities. The Mile End district was already being built up when the Eastern Counties Railway first strode across the East End from Shoreditch to Stratford on miles of grimy brick viaduct. When they built the goods yard it had to be as compact as possible on either side of the viaduct: the Regent's Canal formed the eastern boundary, the Victoria Park cemetery was to the north, the Jews' cemetery on the south side and terraced houses of the 1850s hemmed in the remainder. The difference in level between the goods yard and the viaduct was accomplished by building a steep ramp down from the main line, between the pairs of tracks and then turning the line at the bottom through a right angle to reach the lines on either side. There was a linking tunnel under the main line. Traffic for the yard was extracted from the great Temple Mills Sidings and loaded trucks returned there each day. The stubby little Y4 class 0-4-0 tank engines that worked the yard were known as 'Pots' to the crews. They had to be powerful enough to cope with loads of hundreds of tons on the steep ramp while able to negotiate the sharp bends in the cramped yards, so a short wheelbase was combined with tiny wheels and a powerful boiler by their designer, A. J. Hill of the Great Eastern. On the eve of World War II the yard was a busy service centre for the tightly packed East End industrial community. Shunting went on around the clock, except on Sunday, when the Pot returned to Stratford for a washout and servicing. My father was assigned to the yard as a fireman on a three-shift system. He had every Sunday free and a Saturday off every third week. The task was not over-arduous. A ton of coal had to be shovelled from bunker to firebox, the recoaling and watering done as necessary, and the fire raked and cleaned in the small firebox.

Problems started with the onset of war. The blackout regulations were particularly difficult in the cramped confines of the goods yard, beset with obstructions such as points levers, which were at least painted white, slippery rails, uneven sleepers, puddles of unknown depth and content, and wagons moving under gravity. To make matters worse the quantity of traffic increased as winter approached. Up to sixteen hours a day of the shunting was performed in the dark, the only light coming from dim shaded lanterns and the locomotive cab which was curtained so that the glare of the fire would not be seen from above, making the footplate very claustrophobic. Fogs and smogs were frequent in the low-lying Lea Valley next to the Regent's Canal, but at least in that first winter of the war there was no bombing.

The operating routines worked out in that winter of waiting relied heavily on co-ordination between shunter and fireman, who relayed signals and shouted instructions to the driver. When a trainload of trucks came in from Temple Mills, the shunting engine propelled them to the sidings where they were to be unloaded. Long experience of the yard, knowing every roll and creak of the track, every click of every rail joint, enabled the crew to get the train into position to cut the wagons. The shunters then stationed themselves at the points. The yardmaster peered at each wagon label with his feeble lamp and established how many trucks there were in each cut. A shunter then levered his pole over the buffers and under the coupling chain as the train was buffered up and a deft flick uncoupled the chain, releasing the cut into its appropriate siding. The yardman swung his lamp towards the fireman to indicate the distance to edge forward, then stop again. The freed wagons rolled forward jerkily over the points and were instantly engulfed in darkness. Soon a reassuring crash of steel on steel indicated that the last cut had arrived and all was clear for the next. Then the next cut blundered forward and so on until the little engine drew abreast of the shunters, who could climb aboard for a brew-up before tackling the next load.

Extracting wagons to assemble a train for Temple Mills required finer judgement as the engine had to go down pitch dark sidings and halt inches from the wagons so that the shunter could couple up, check the brakes and signal for the Pot to reverse and then propel the wagons into an assembly siding. The fireman positioned on the lowest step of the locomotive strained his eyes in the gloom to relay the lamp signals. Illness and call-up reduced the labour force that winter, and sometimes the shunters were forced to operate with the lamp on one arm and the shunting pole in the other hand, yet they became so adept that there were few accidents, and only snow and ice really slowed down the round of shunting.

After a year of blackout without bombs, Devonshire Street yard and the whole East End suddenly had to cope with pandemonium. The bombing started in earnest on Saturday 7 September 1940 after a night of continuous alerts. The final shift of the week signed on at 2.00pm that day. After finishing they were due to take the Pot back to Stratford and return home. The Underground to Liverpool Street was operating but Roman Road and Commercial Road were blocked to bus traffic as fire engines and ambulances from all over London were called in to help after the first bombs fell. My father had to walk the last couple of miles and try to cope with the new situation. The carriage sidings just up the line were hit and carriages set alight. Fortunately most were rescued. Incendiary bombs had to be smothered by shunters and footplate crew the moment they flared. Old sacks, buckets of sand, stirrup pumps, tarpaulins, anything to hand was used, usually effectively. On a later occasion the fires got a hold on the trucks in the north yard at Devonshire Street, hemming in the engine crew on both sides with flames. The only escape was to dive into the Regent's Canal and then swim and wade to the south side of the viaduct and safety. The Pot was only singed and things could have been much worse.

While the civilian population sought shelter in the new Central Line tunnel under Bethnal Green and at points west, the railwaymen carried on under fire. Shifts lasted as long as it took for relief crews to reach the yard. Journeys to and from work after dark became a nightmare. A local train from Mile End or Bethnal Green to Liverpool Street could be stopped by a raid for an hour or more as inflammable wooden sleepers burned and the rails spread, whilst wooden wagons and carriages were a perpetual hazard. Proceeding under caution soon became the practice with the train crawling along so that a sudden stop could be made if the track gave way. The Widened Lines section of the Underground was the most vulnerable and suffered several closures, so father preferred the Central and Bakerloo lines route to reach Edgware Road from Liverpool Street. The platforms were a dense mass of dozing humanity, although the gradual introduction of bunk beds tidied up the initial mess. When the raids were really bad and the journey home by train or bike seemed too lethal, the shunters' hut provided a haven for the footplate crews. A bench and a blanket after a can of hot tea to wash down toast and dripping was preferable to any of the alternatives. Ack-ack guns shook the whole of St John's Wood when they fired from the top of Primrose Hill and made sleep at home impossible. The long walk to Liverpool Street in the dark was very hazardous and there was no certainty of trains late in the evening, whereas there was always warmth and company in the yard; the latter was very important in the absence of family.

The real domestic disruptions started late in May 1940, immediately after the evacuation of Dunkirk. The author's school was evacuated from Paddington to Hayle in Cornwall *en bloc*, and with daily threat of invasion, blitz and worse, mother and sister were sent down at the end of the month to stay with relations, while father carried on in the East End goods yard at Devonshire Street and had a long weekend to visit us every sixth week.

Bomb shelters were erected in the courtyards. They were never tested, for when the railway flats received a direct hit from a V1 flying bomb in 1944 they were out of use and yet unharmed, while a few yards away thirty-seven died and over one hundred were injured. During the blitz, conditions for the railway staff became very difficult. Journeys to and from work were a nightmare. The Metropolitan line to Liverpool Street was particularly badly hit, so my father cycled where possible. Bomb craters, streets littered with debris, hosepipes, and shrapnel were all regular hazards of dark night-shift journeys. Sleep was at best fitful in a lonely flat against the sound of air-raid sirens, shuddering blasts from near and far, and strange lights in green, blue and orange which lit up the sky from time to time. Entertainment largely closed down for several months, most of the children and many of the mothers had been evacuated, so life was very strained and strange until the bombing petered out in May 1941.

Plans for the family to be reunited were delayed by the arrival of a little brother in July 1941. A two-roomed flat for a family of five was almost impossible to cope with, as a cramped reunion at Christmas proved. Top to tail sleeping arrangements could be borne for a few days, but three rooms were vital. These became vacant in the spring of 1942, two blocks away. The rent was 15/-a week on a wage with overtime of about £4 a week. Frequent illness of mother and children incurred heavy doctor's bills. After the healthy air of Cornwall the grime of London, the nits and worms picked up at school, the depressingly war-battered neighbourhood, repelled us as London struggled back to some semblance of normality. Bombing was rare, but the blackout, ruins and shortages of most things made life difficult at the very least, but the black market run by railwaymen partially relieved some of the shortages. One of the ticket collectors at Baker Street was selling china dolls' heads, one of which was the basis of my sister's beloved only doll. Footplatemen who went into country areas returned with otherwise unobtainable luxuries such as fresh (well, quite fresh) eggs, rabbits and animals that just happened to get in the way of their engine. Stratford shunters who worked down to the docks appeared to be able to get their hands on almost anything, but mother shied away from that sort of thing and told father to have nothing to do with it; her word was law.

The Germans made life difficult again in the summer of 1944. The first V1 landed a couple of hundred yards up the line from father's yard, demolishing the viaduct at Grove Road, Bow, and putting the line to Liverpool Street out of action for several days. Another struck the signal-box at nearby Marylebone station and the regular scream of the 'doodle-bugs' overhead, followed by a horrible silence and then an explosion became part of everyday life. School was largely conducted in the reinforced cellars but father went on with his work according to the shift schedule, the milkround that I helped on still flourished and mother did her best to keep things calm. When sirens sounded we had an orderly routine of crawling under the Victorian brass bedstead and burying our heads in soft materials. When the V1 struck, father was at work. The children had just been called in for supper late after a sunny August evening and mother was quietly ironing a pile of whites, preparing for the start of school term. The windows imploded, all the doors were wrenched off their hinges, glass was strewn everywhere, upholstery ripped to pieces, curtains and blackout in shreds, yet we were completely unharmed. Clouds of dust drifted in through the gaping windows, then shouts came from the stairwell: 'Turn the gas out! Are you alright? Switch that . . . light out'. The ARP and the police had arrived, a later report said within two minutes, although it seemed like two hours, so sudden was our change in fortune.

During the V-bomb attack on London there was a complete

ban on any reports on the radio or in the press, so when father walked up Lisson Grove about two hours after, he was verging on a nervous breakdown the nearer he got to home. Fire engines, police cars, ambulances and crowds of helpers and sightseers were picked out by arc lights, all the more unusual since a strict blackout was in force elsewhere. As he picked his way over the rubble and felt his way up the stairs, he later admitted to the greatest foreboding since there were no lights on in the block, despite the lack of curtains. Mother had refused to go to a rest centre, so we were reunited at the first possible moment. Temporary repairs were made, but damage was so extensive that father arranged for our re-evacuation to Cornwall as soon as possible for the autumn.

An uncle who had been working as a yardman was killed while shepherding the children after the siren sounded, as was a friend with whom I had been playing shortly before. Most of our neighbours were cut or bruised; the one above us had concussion when the gas meter landed on his head. It was as well to bear such incidents in mind when trains were late or did not run at all during that dreadful summer. Railwaymen of all grades were managing as best they could under terrifying strain. Would their families be alive? Would the track explode in front of them? Would the V1 whose motor had just stopped explode too close? Yet they carried on and most of the trains ran.

Not only the running side was in danger. Ashford works in Kent was also in the front line. That vital engineering centre received no less than 2,881 red warnings of imminent attack, yet under fire it was more productive than before or since. The Q1 austerity engine, LMS-designed class 8Fs, wagons, munitions, breakdown trains, repairs and refits were carried out on a massive scale. Figures like 1,600 12 ton wagons assembled in three months during 1941 were being achieved, while the factory Home Guard was manning a roof-top anti-aircraft gun to protect the works. Locomotive construction at Brighton works was resumed to relieve the overstretched Eastleigh and keep the busiest lines in the country going.

At the end of the war tired men and women were still running an overworked system. The busiest lines had seen traffic increases many times their pre-war level. The footplate was still a male stronghold, but the ladies had done a much wider range of jobs than in World War I. Attitudes of both sexes were generally co-operative when the pressures were on and railway staff rose magnificently to challenges. No trains were abandoned under fire, there were heroic incidents of sacrifice, as at Soham when the driver of a bomb train that caught fire sacrificed his life in trying to move the dangerous cargo out of the station before it exploded. Management drove itself remorselessly, often working over eighty hours a week for months on end, but as pressures eased late in 1944, so some attitudes changed.

In the last months of the war the cleaners at King's Cross shed were still women recruited during the war. They objected to cleaning underneath engines, where the inside motions dripped oil on their turbans and where contact with the caked grime smeared their make-up. There was only one temptation that would get them under and that was the mixture of violet oil and ether that was put into the middle big end to indicate to the driver by smell if it was overheating. Any left over from refilling that Achilles' heel of the LNER's Gresley engines was dabbed liberally on the gentle lady cleaners. Problems arose when they toasted themselves before their mess-room stove and the pungent vapours filled the air, but it was cheaper than Woolworth's scent, if you could get it.

Men and women had worked full shifts, given up holidays, joined the Home Guard or other auxiliary services, rendered first aid and attended classes in all manner of war-related tasks. Poorly maintained machinery was coaxed to perform near miracles and there was little industrial strife for the duration. However, when the scent of victory became established there was a relaxation. Some of the dog-tired managers started to complain that full discipline could not be enforced as alternative jobs were becoming available. A work-force that had had little leisure or proper holidays for over five years started to become restive, especially the temporary elements in it. The new mood was reinforced when voting patterns changed the government in the summer of 1945, bringing to power a Labour government with the nationalisation of the railways as part of its programme.

# 8
## Line, Shed and Yard

The train crews have the glamour jobs but working to support their efforts is a vast, indispensable and almost unseen body of railwaymen to maintain the track, prepare and marshal the trains in the sidings and goods yards and signal them safely along their journey.

The track used by the major British railways until recently, and still very much in evidence on quieter lines and sidings, consisted of steel rails weighing nearly 1 cwt to the yard, held to sleepers by cast-iron chairs, or if flat bottomed by Pandrol clips. The track is set in packed stone chipping ballast from quarries at Nuneaton, Meldon and Shap, although furnace slag, flints, gravel and other less satisfactory material can still be found. Track suffers great vertical and lateral stresses from the passage of trains, especially on curves or at major changes in gradient, and the keys and clips holding it in place also come loose. Steel also fractures and bends, sometimes unexpectedly, so that regular inspection and maintenance are absolutely essential to safe running. Depending on the number of lines and amount of traffic, each short section had a gang of platelayers consisting of a ganger and three to four lengthsmen who were based in a hut, usually of brick or later of pre-cast concrete. They walked the line daily, checking the gauge, tightening screws, knocking in oak keys, packing ballast under sinking sleepers with the aid of jacks and shovels, and used a riddle to make sure that the new ballast was clean and would drain well. All drains along the section were checked to make sure there was no blockage which might cause flooding. Overhanging trees were trimmed, as were hedges that survived the fires started by sparks from thrashed engines. Grass was cut by hand on the sides of cuttings and embankments, lest it become long and be set alight by incandescent cinders. For the majority of platelayers the job was similar to farmwork: open air and requiring a lot of strength, but rather better paid and with none of the peaks and troughs of harvest and winter. The cabin not only stored lifting jacks, riddles, shovels and gauges, but was also the place to relax. A stove fed with stray nuggets of coal, lopped branches and dead wood or old sleepers made a cosy little den. Pheasants and rabbits were regularly lying on the tracks after an unwary crossing of the lines, so together with potatoes often growing wild alongside the line, or within leaning distance of it in fields, hot lunches were no problem. When combined with a crossing-keeper's cottage manned by a wife, life could be pleasant indeed. Certificates were regularly awarded to those keeping the best sections of track, signed by the engineer and countersigned by the section inspector.

A much larger gang manned the ballast trains which undertook large-scale renewals. Old wagons and carriages with mess facilities, even sleeping bunks in remoter areas of Scotland, catered for gangs of between twenty to thirty men who were needed in pre-mechanised days, working at weekends and in times of slack traffic. The basic need was to dig out the old ballast, sieve out the crushed stone and then add new stone to the best of the old, repack and relay as required. Steam cranes were used from early in the century by the larger companies to speed track work, but manual methods were used until after national-isation in remoter areas. All sorts and conditions of men joined these roving gangs: Irish navvies, fishermen in winter, foot-loose ex-servicemen, for the work was rough and the accommodation sometimes even rougher.

Both types of crew required an eye kept open for trains which, as a number of tragedies show, could run an unwary gang down with horrific results. The ganger and his lengthsmen knew the timetable by heart and were sent notices of special trains. They also developed a sixth sense, while one of their number would frequently scan in both directions to make absolutely sure. With larger gangs a lookout was appointed, armband and brass horn distinguishing him from the rest. The train crews were informed, the foreman ganger had a timetable and amendments, and speed limits and warnings were usually posted, but even when the gang stood clear in the 'eight foot' between double tracks, jostling or swaying loose fittings on trains, or bottles and the like flung from windows could still maim or kill. The job was very dangerous in the early years of this century when a hundred platelayers a year were killed and even more injured. They represented about a quarter of all those killed on the railways.

The most dangerous time for platelayers was during fog, but they were also expected to be on duty during snowy conditions to keep points clear, water cranes in action and undertake a myriad of other jobs, so they were certainly not fair-weather workers. An example of this occurred in the dreadful winter of 1947 when there were six weeks of Arctic weather, especially bad on the exposed north Norfolk coast where platelayer Hugh McLeod was on duty at East Runton Junction with crowbar and brazier keeping the points open. Visibility was nil when the train left Cromer Beach station for Mundesley and North Walsham after twenty-four hours of snow. Plateplayer McLeod was knocked down and killed without the driver being aware of it, and only after the signalman grew worried when he did not appear for his break was his body discovered. Such was the price of running the trains.

Fogs were much more prevalent in the London of the 1950s then they are now. Railway pollution at busy junctions made things locally even worse. As there was no automatic train control on the Great Northern system, double block working was introduced under these conditions. This meant that there was to be only one train in two blocks at any one time. The telegraph lad would be sent to Finsbury Park station to see that trains did not start when they could not see the advanced signal for the slow line. No 5 would offer the train to Harringay box, which would refuse to accept it, Finsbury Park noting offer and refusal in the block book. Harringay would then offer the train to Hornsey No 1 and if they were free to accept it, then Harringay would accept the train, which was now free to leave Finsbury Park station. Naturally this meant delays on winter nights, but at least it was safe.

The safest mode of travel in Britain is by rail, far safer than car, aeroplane or even Shanks's pony. Part of the reason for the excellent safety record, at least in this century, has been the constant improvement of equipment, especially the braking systems and the track, but the inbuilt safety of the signalling system is what allows British trains to move confidently in nearly all types of weather without the massive headlights and constant whistle-blowing that characterises train travel in North America and many other parts of the world. These factors, plus an enclosed track, have built up that enviable safety record, achieved largely with the type of manual signalling that still persists over long stretches of our railway system and which has been the mainstay of British signalling practice for over a century. It is this traditional type of signalling on which most of our present-day signalmen were trained that occupies us here, rather than the later computerised systems that control dozens of miles of track.

Signalling first evolved on the Liverpool & Manchester Railway in the 1830s when increased speed, allied to inadequate braking systems, came up against an increase of traffic that demanded some regulations to avoid serious accidents. Within a few years of making the first rules, the LNWR had produced a section on signalling in its Rules and Regulations illustrating what the driver would see and how he should respond.

Semaphores gradually replaced the flag-waving policeman, but the problem of finding out what was happening at stations on either side was not so easily dealt with. The solution to signalling problems and also to those raised by single-line working were solved by W. F. Cooke on the Yarmouth & Norwich Railway which opened in 1844. He used a single-needle telegraph

### HAND SIGNALS.

Men required to give Hand Signals are provided with Red, Green, and White Flags, and a Signal Lamp, with Red, Green, and White Glasses, and with Fog Signals; but in any emergency, when not provided with those means of signalling, the following are adopted, namely,—

The ALL RIGHT SIGNAL is shown by extending the arm horizontally, so as to be distinctly seen by the Engine-driver, thus—

The CAUTION SIGNAL, to Proceed Slowly, is shown by one arm held straight up, thus—

The STOP SIGNAL is shown by holding both arms straight up, thus, or by waving any object with violence—

Manual signalling by railway police, ancestor of the signalman

instrument showing which section of the line was occupied and in which direction the train was going.

The electric telegraph appeared at about the same time and greatly aided communication between stations, followed in the 1850s by the invention of bell communication between stations. These relatively simple devices and systems were usually adequate in the early years of railways, but they did not eliminate human error, as the Thorpe disaster of 1874, on the line from Norwich to Yarmouth, so eloquently showed. A mistake in receiving the signals from the Cooke instrument resulted in two trains setting off from either end of the Norwich–Brundall block section, resulting in a head-on collision.

Blocks of points and signals varying in length from a few hundred yards to several miles punctuated the main lines out of the major London stations. Fast expresses, suburban steam trains, local stopping trains, loose-coupled and vacuum-fitted goods trains, light engines, and an occasional runaway, all moved at different speeds over a spaghetti bowl of lines, hauled by temperamental steam engines which could and regularly did throw the best designed timetable into utter confusion. The system therefore demanded great feats of understanding and ingenuity on the part of signalmen to keep the traffic moving, regardless of the exigencies of weather, breakdowns or other causes.

In country areas, signalmen were often recruited from porters and other station staff who had learned their signalling by helping run the box in times of great pressure, thus becoming porter-signalmen, a first step to greater things. In the London area and other places with dense networks of lines and myriad points and junctions, the divorce between station work and signal-box work was almost complete, so trainee signalmen were recruited from lads who had learned their craft as telegraph boys and who had undergone a course in one of the training schools.

Finsbury Park No 5 box was one of the group of seven guarding the approaches to King's Cross, a manual box with 55 levers in the frame and a typical Great Northern Railway design with a barge-board gabled roof. Over the frame there were the block instruments, linking the box to other signalmen up and down the line, and a diagram showing the points and signals controlled by the signal frame. A cupboard filled with stationery, detonators and other railway miscellanea stood next to the door, together with a small gas stove for cooking meals, in addition to an enclosed fire whose flue penetrated the roof. A chair and a table were provided for doing the paperwork, while the telegraph lad had to be content with a high stool, but a former occupant had donated an elderly but comfortable armchair, where a well-earned rest could be taken during traffic lulls.

The key document was the block book in which details and times of every train that entered the block were listed. Timing was taken from a big-faced LNER clock which was synchronised every day, but very seldom lost time. Telephones and telegraph instruments, a paraffin store and toilet completed the appointments of the box. Unlike its neighbours, it was not track circuited, which led to doubts about trains clearing the points in foggy weather; more leg work for the telegraph lad!

The interlocking of points with signals, refinements in single-line working and further use of electricity with the introduction of track circuiting, finally eliminated most of the human errors attributable to signalmen, but driver error through ignoring signals is still unfortunately with us, as a 1979 collision at Paisley demonstrated when a driver took his train past a red signal and hit another at a junction. However, accidents involving injury or loss of life to passengers are fortunately very rare, thanks to the procedures and the careful work of signalmen in the boxes along the major railway arteries of Britain, or in the electronic control rooms which are taking over from them.

Signal-boxes on busy lines have to be kept open around the clock on every day, except over the Christmas holiday, which has been no easy task in most of the post-war years when full employment and unsocial hours have made life elsewhere seem easier. Any closure of a box through illness, absence or holidays slows up the flow of traffic greatly by extending the length of the block and therefore of the time taken by a train to pass through it. Consequently the railways have in this century employed a large body of relief signalmen who are ready to go to any box in their district and take over with little or no notice. Such experienced men need to be rapid learners as on one day they might be in a main-line box such as Leicester North, the next controlling a passing loop on a minor line, then somewhere else on the system. Such a relief man learns that no two boxes have identical problems, even those next to each other on a main line. Each set of levers and their diagrams has to be learned immediately, together with any local routing bell codes so that there can be instant reaction to messages. A new timetable has to be learned and planning undertaken for the shift so that breaks can be taken without interruptions to traffic.

Such breaks for signalmen and platelayers tended to be frugal when working in emergency conditions. Rule 83, Clause B of the Appendix to Rules stated: 'Whilst it is necessary that the men should be supplied with a good meal, it is essential that the greatest economy should be used and care taken that there is no waste and the most suitable refreshments are bread and cheese'.

A newcomer to a signal-box with no knowledge of signalling would find the whole process and medley of bells, morse and telephone conversations so baffling as to wonder how any services ever got through, let alone relatively smoothly. The lad fresh out of school took months to learn the job fully, doing first the simpler tasks, then going to the signalling school in Hatfield (on the LNER) where he was taught how to send and receive messages. By practising on model layouts, the functions of each part of the box gradually became clear, so that on return to his home box, he was a much more useful member of staff, able to deputise briefly, fill in the block book correctly and start to communicate with other boxes intelligently. He did not work on the night shift, but it still meant rising at 5.00am for the early shift.

Over the months, the routine became familiar. The bell system was learned so thoroughly that on hearing 3-1, three strokes-pause-one stroke, the words 'suburban passenger train' registered almost without thought. Other messages such as 'accepted train now entering section' would be acted on and written up without further ado, while the seven strokes continuously of 'stop and examine' would result instantly in all signals being put on danger, for instance after the previous signalman had noticed a door open or a hotbox. There were some thirty bell signals in all used in the area from King's Cross to Wood Green and once learned, they were a speedy and accurate way of communicating up and down the line.

The levers in the box worked the signals and points by means of wires and rods. As these were made of metal, cold weather shrank them and hot weather expanded them, sometimes resulting in the action of the lever not being reciprocated at the other end. As the box was in view of almost all the points and signals that it controlled, a visual check sufficed; but in misty weather, if the box was not equipped with signal and point repeaters, confirming electrically that the required change had in fact taken place, the telegraph lad had to make a check on the spot when the signalman could feel his lever become very stiff and not complete its movement in the frame. A broom and a crowbar were the usual tools for clearing any obstruction, and a can of oil also helped in hot weather when lubricating oil tended to evaporate. In really cold weather, it was the general practice to move all points and signals every hour and give attention to those that showed signs of sticking. Any more vigorous action might result in broken wires and rods.

Signalmen are and were less directly supervised than most railwaymen, thanks to the nature of their job. Unofficial items of uniform, such as carpet slippers, and comfortable additions to the spartan official furniture of the box were generally tolerated. Accordingly there were plenty of opportunities for some signalmen to develop eccentricities, so long as they did not delay the trains or come to the notice of headquarters. One such character was Herbie Fox of Haywards Heath, a 22 stone bachelor who had to move sideways in the narrower parts of boxes he served. One of his relief jobs was at Ardingly on the now defunct branch to Horsted Keynes. Between signalling the occasional branch train, his job with the regular signalman at the end of term of the nearby Ardingly College was to label and load hundreds of trunks, tuck boxes and cases for the departing boarders. The job done manually had usually taken the men five days of twelve-hour shifts. If they did it faster then the time off was theirs for the taking. Herbie achieved it in two and a half days, which set the stationmaster at Haywards Heath wondering, so on the verge of retirement he asked the signalman how he managed it. 'Oh, that's simple guv'nor, I always hired a fork lift truck', was the reply.

Time to nip off from main-line signalling duties was not so forthcoming with the close interval service on the Brighton line. On lightly trafficked lines, collusion was sometimes possible on manual lines where neighbouring boxes would look after the traffic for a few minutes and fend off enquiries. Herbie was single and to do his shopping on a Saturday morning, he arranged with his mate to drive to each of the shops in turn and quickly get back to the signal-box to pull the levers for the next train. On one memorable morning best forgotten, the errant pair spotted the stationmaster coming in the opposite direction while cruising down the high street at 25mph. They both ducked so as not to be seen, bobbed up again seconds later, whizzed around the block and got back to the box in double-quick time. Half an hour later the stationmaster visited the box and was offered his usual cup of 'Orange Label' tea to which they were both partial.

'By the way, Herbie, I've just seen your car in town', said the stationmaster.

'Oh yes', said Herbie, 'I often lend it to a friend while I'm at work, he has a spare key.'

'Funny thing, there didn't seem to be anybody in it, Herbie.'

'Ah, that must have been because he's not very tall.'

His accomplice in the corner choked on his mug of tea and was glad that Herbie was suddenly preoccupied with a rush of trains. A heart attack forced Herbie to diet down to 15 stone and go on to platform duties, much to his distaste. He later died of the same complaint, to be remembered by the commuters with a plaque on the station, a rare tribute which could be repeated elsewhere with good effects on passenger/staff relationships.

Things were rather different in signal-boxes around the great cities and where manual signalling remained, its operation was extremely intricate.

For example the approaches to King's Cross were amongst the most congested and poorly designed of any London terminal

127

before the replanning and diversion of local trains in the early 1980s. The series of long, steeply graded tunnels interspersed with goods yards, locomotive sheds and carriage siding junctions, together with the maze of lines at Finsbury Park, made it an operational nightmare. The traffic situation changed frequently during the day, even without any problems arising, and this was reflected in the pattern of work at Finsbury Park No 5 box.

The signalman and telegraph lad relieved the night shift at 6.00am and for the next two hours they dealt with the traffic between north London and Hither Green, Norwood and Stewart's Lane, all south of the river. The route was over the Widened Lines from King's Cross to Blackfriars. The trains came in from Temple Mills or Royal Docks to Ferme Park goods yard, between Finsbury Park and Harringay, ready to leave when a path was clear for them. Often they were so long that they filled all the one local and four arrival roads there, preventing the departure of goods trains for the north. The southbound trains had to be cleared to make room for goods trains from the south. After 7.00am the empty sleeping cars and carriages of the overnight trains started to come up from King's Cross, bound for Hornsey or Bounds Green where they were cleaned and stabled for the departure the same evening. Early morning commuter stock from the Finsbury Park sidings had to go down to King's Cross or straight to its turnround point at Hertford, with cross-currents to Moorgate and Broad Street, Hitchin and Hatfield. Amid this toing and froing, express passenger trains in and out of the terminal were but a small part of the total traffic, while light engines were dealt with as necessary, although they usually moved quickly and caused few problems.

The morning rush subsided soon after Train 50, known to most people as the *Flying Scotsman*, had passed a few minutes after 10.00am. It was time to put the kettle on the gas ring and warm up the sausage rolls. The remaining hours of duty were relatively light after the hurly-burly of the first four hours and work settled down to a steady rhythm of expresses in and out, a regular pattern of locals, interspersed by goods trains, and light engines. The first two hours of the late shift followed the same pattern. The only crucial judgement that had to be made was the path of the class C goods train from King's Cross Top Yard to the north which followed the 3.00pm express if that was on time, but if late, then the fast goods would have to use the slow line until overtaken by the express.

The evening rush started at 4.00pm and continued until 6.30pm, so tea had to be early, since there was no time for any relaxation once the pressure was on. Expresses were leaving King's Cross at five minute intervals on the fast line, while locals came in as quickly as they could, puffing up from the depths of the City or over the house-tops from Broad Street. There was much activity at Finsbury Park as some locals started from there, connecting with others from the London termini. If there was late running, the connection was held, thus blocking a badly needed line, causing some friction between box and station, as well as creating delays up the line. One train received what appeared to be preferential treatment, being double-headed from King's Cross to Finsbury Park and so suffering none of the delays due to slipping and failure in Gasworks Tunnel. It was rumoured that an important personage used this train regularly. Goods workings were kept to a minimum in the early evening, so after checking that the block book was up to date and that train control had been kept informed of any delays, a welcome kettle of hot water was produced soon after 6.30pm before the evening goods trains and empty stock workings again demanded the full attention of signalman and telegraph lad.

When chaos reigned at King's Cross, the breaks would be cut short or sacrificed altogether. Rerouting of trains, cancellation for various reasons, or extra stops required many messages to be handled, track routing to be changed and traffic control told at all times, so signalman and telegraph lad were on the go the whole time. Great annoyance was caused when anyone along the chain forgot to inform others of a change, but such mistakes were inevitable given the density of the traffic and the scarcity of alternative paths.

Work was never boring or even lonely at Finsbury Park No 5. At times it also had its lighter side. As the night sleeper trains came into King's Cross, some passengers appeared to be under the illusion that they could not be seen about their toilet and dressing, but telegraph messages of a very unofficial kind were winging their way southwards: 'Look in third coach of train accepted' from Harringay might reveal a sight to gladden the heart of a signalman who had left his own bed at an unearthly hour. Some messages were not recorded in the block book.

It will be many years yet before manual signalling of this type is finally abolished. Its worth has been proven and its safety factors increased over a century and more, but it is very labour intensive. Behind the crews manning the boxes night and day stand reliefs to cover illness and accidents, signal engineers to keep the wires, rods and pulleys working smoothly, and platelayers who keep the points in good order. There is a little friendly ragging between box and platelayer at times. Bobby Whatley, the Finsbury Park signalman, had a game trying to catch the oil brush of a platelayer in the points as he was lubricating them, but the only time he ever succeeded was by accident for there is always a split second warning when manual points are about to be moved. Junctions, sidings, manual boxes and ground frames have been removed by the hundred in the last two decades, resulting in a great exodus of signalmen from railway service, but the comfort and convenience of an electronic switchboard is of benefit to those who work the new systems. The manual box belongs to the age of steam, but contrives to outlive it.

Platelayers and signalmen saw to the smooth running of trains, but much of the performance of the engines themselves depended on the skill and devotion of the shed staff. At the apex of the pyramid was the shedmaster, a character as variable as one could hope to find. Management trainees in their early twenties sometimes occupied the post while others were grizzled sexagenarians who maintained the 'god in a bowler hat' outlook to staff and visitors alike. The certainties were that they were overworked, looking after an often superannuated fleet of engines in addition to the human vagaries of their staff, definitely underpaid for the hours they usually put in and ingenious in maintaining a service against all the odds in the post-war period. Of the small clerical staff the typist/telephonist and the roster clerk often had pride of place: the former kept angry callers and visitors at bay until a suitable occasion could be found; the latter, if competent, would make the running staff's lives easier by fitting in shifts to suit domestic and traffic conditions, without upsetting seniority patterns or stranding men or machines in distant places at unsuitable hours. The person who could perform such miracles was a treasure beyond valuation and needed to be humoured, cajoled and otherwise made to feel wanted, needed and happy.

The running foreman or foremen and the foremen in charge of fitters and labourers worked closely with the shedmaster, deputising for him in his absence. The fitting crew with their labourers and sometimes apprentices, did the day-to-day maintenance and repairs on the engines where they stood if they were minor. If they needed further examination, sheer legs were provided in many sheds, and larger ones acted as regional repair shops for the smaller sheds. Old Oak Common did jobs for Southall, Slough and other local sheds that they could not manage themselves through lack of equipment. Preventive examination played a large part in keeping the wheels rolling. Drivers' reports of knocking or other unusual sounds were followed up at once to prevent further deterioration, while the mileage was also noted so that routine replacement of worn parts could be made before they gave trouble. The wide variety of engine types was a grave hindrance in most sheds, usually resulting in the stores either having a very wide variety of spares or sometimes not having a spare at all and the engine being out of order until one could be found or made. Many tricks were resorted to in order to get around this problem: filing down larger sizes or borrowing the needed part from an engine due to go into shops or on re-allocation elsewhere. A good storekeeper would stock up with far more than needed so as not to be caught short. Past experience taught that some items were produced in small batches, and then nothing for a long while, or another item was likely to fail in large numbers when the weather changed. Storekeepers and fitters had a mutual interest in remaining good friends.

Boilersmiths and their confederates regarded themselves as a separate group. The chief boilersmith had a hard and noisy life, riveting, patching, testing and lagging. Older ones tended to be rather deaf and short of breath – industrial diseases that were once regarded as part of the job. One of the filthiest jobs was blasting the firetubes with compressed air. Although an industrial mask was provided in later years, a wet handkerchief over the nose and mouth was more normal. Sand and coke dust was inevitably breathed in and silicosis often resulted.

Only the larger, modernised sheds such as Carnforth, Norwich and Exmouth Junction boasted great concrete coaling towers which operated automatically. Others, including Old Oak Common, relied on coaling with small iron tubs, often hand-loaded from four-wheeled trucks. The cloud of dust raised each time a ton of coal crashed into tender or bunker made this job as mucky as mining, despite regular hosing of the coal stage and coal. The many varieties of coal and their burning qualities were known both to driver and coal-stage foreman. Best-quality Welsh steam coal was usually kept for express locomotives as it could cost three times as much as Yorkshire coals in the east of the country. Quarrelling with this foreman was not to be recommended, as he could quite easily include a ton or two of duff in a big tender and bury it under better coal, since it was usual for the crew to leave the engine during coaling.

When flare lamps illuminated cabs and the internal motions of engines, when oil was carried on the engine in large tin cannisters, when prickers and bent darts needed maintenance or brick arches inside fireboxes needed rebuilding, the humble tinsmith was on hand to do the job. In larger sheds there was a blacksmith and bricklayer as well to share the numerous tasks, but in depots allocated with about a score of engines, the tinsmith was truly the jack of all trades and master of many of them.

Keeping everything tidy by wheelbarrowing ashes away, hosing down, sweeping messrooms, tidying coal heaps and generally doing what they were asked were the shed labourers, some of whom were demoted from footplate work or a more skilled task which, through injury or inability, they could no longer perform. The sheer volume of muck – oily, dusty, gritty, muddy or slushy – was always a nightmare to shedmasters. Victorian guv'nors would sometimes get it put into the nearest river after dark, but when oily waste from Stratford ignited the Channelsea River, it was evident that such methods were frowned on for having offended the eleventh commandment: 'Thou shalt not get caught'. The major problem was ash disposal: paths were filled in with it, farmers used ash to lighten heavy clay soils, landfill sites could use it by the truckload – anything to get rid of it. Certainly in locomotive and goods yards a thick layer of well-bedded ash made the going easier and the footholds firmer.

Some of the dangers of railway yards have already been pointed out, for shunters were most at risk, and in blackout conditions the situation was even more dangerous. The complexity of a national railway system with wagonload goods trains, the norm until recently, demanded that trains be split and reassembled at numerous points on the railway system. Names like Tinsley, March, Severn Tunnel Junction and Erimus (Middlesbrough) were as familiar to goods guards and their footplate colleagues as Waverley and Exeter St Davids were to passenger crews. Originally each company had its own yards at each major junction, leading to confusion and numerous small yards, each fed by trip runs from other yards in the town as well as from trains entering directly from main or branch lines. The clink and chuff of shunting at all hours was a constant background noise in Crewe, Carlisle, York and Newport to name but a few major junctions, which were also major freight interchanges. A swathe of north-west London from Cricklewood, through Neasden to Willesden and Acton, was very similar. Lengthy coal trains were broken up and sent to smaller yards dotting the metropolis. Until the 1960s most of these trains were of 10 or 12 ton open, loose-coupled wagons. By sorting and resorting they eventually reached their unloading point; so very different from today's block trains.

Hump yards, where trains to be sorted were pushed up a gradient by a massive tank engine – usually eight-coupled – so that the wagons could be sorted into sidings by gravity, were the quickest way of breaking up and reassembling the trucks. A modern yard like March, with track retarders to slow the descending truck, made the shunter's life much easier. A well-lit yard with wagons all going into their right tracks at moderate speeds, no retrievals to slow down and foul up the work, dry underfoot and a smart getaway could even make the job pleasurable. But frosty weather, slippery conditions underfoot, jammed brakes, poor checking, hard-to-read labels and the attenuation of the process could be mind-numbing. Yet despite the importance of the traffic and the much greater hardships suffered by yardmen, shunting engine drivers and goods guards, they were lowly rated in the railway hierarchy. Despite this, the skills they displayed were of a very high order, some of them not in the Rule Book, others specifically forbidden by it. Fly-shunting at Melton Constable was commonplace under the M&GN regime, right under the gaze of the engineer. An incoming goods train would arrive and as it approached the points where the train was to be divided it was braked sharply, causing the wagons to buffer-up, enabling the shunter to detach the engine, which would then accelerate forward on to its road, while the wagons would come forward more slowly and be cut into the Norwich, Cromer and Yarmouth roads as required. Quick reading of the wagon labels was needed, while the wristwork of the shunter and pointsman had to be deft indeed to avoid nasty accidents. The object was to save time, but an annual death toll amongst shunters of over a hundred until well into the present century makes one think that there must have been better ways of organising their duties.

The growth of train load goods services has eliminated most of the yards noted above. Such trains have a long history. Fish and fruit specials were run in Victorian times when sufficient tonnage was on offer. The obligation to carry made it necessary to run some very diverse trains that were labour intensive, dangerous and slow until the gradual reduction and elimination of loose-coupled wagon load workings.

# 9
## *Union Matters*

Trade-union activity was permitted by law a year before the opening of the Stockton & Darlington Railway, yet it was not until the 1880s that large, stable unions became effective, and only in the present century did the railway companies officially recognise the unions as negotiating agents for its work-force. Even then there was uneasy confrontation between management and unions right up to the present. The threefold division of enginemen, clerical staff and the rest of the railwaymen has been with us for almost a century, reflecting deeply felt differences in status and, in former times, of pay.

In the early years of railway growth there were relatively few periods of industrial action – less than a score before 1870 and each restricted to a single company. In most cases they were repressed with great ferocity by the employment of blacklegs. The Eastern Counties Railway replaced striking enginemen with others recruited from other railways in 1850 and then published a full list of strikers 'who resigned their situations on the 12th of August 1850', circulating it to other railways to ensure that they were not re-employed. Some directors appear to have been genuinely hurt at the apparent disloyalty of railway servants.

In the absence of effective unions, railwaymen aired their grievances through the medium of the 'Memorial', termed by Joseph Tatlow an 'appeal unto Caesar'. In his case the clerical staff at Derby worked from 9.00am until 6.00pm or later, as was often required. The clerical staff in all the offices got up a petition and forwarded it to 'the highest quarters. The boon was granted, and I remember the wave of delight that swept over us, and how we enjoyed the long summer evenings.' They had had an hour knocked off their day with no loss of pay. This was the ideal of a reasonable request being met by direct application, but for the less articulate enginemen and other grades there was need of an intermediary who could discuss conditions cogently and write good English while not embroiling the men in costly strikes.

Until 1880, when the Employers' Liability Act was passed, the railway companies were able to extract an indemnity from their staff, freeing them from claims in cases of injury or accident. Yet the railways were horrifyingly dangerous places of work. The annual Parliamentary 'Return of the Number & Nature of the Accidents & the Injuries to Life and Limb which have occurred on the Railways of Great Britain & Ireland', showed that it was indeed third only to coal-mining and the merchant marine as a lethal occupation, with shunters, enginemen and guards the most at risk. Directors and management who made the reports were seemingly convinced that it was due to staff inattention that most accidents happened. A typical sample from 1851 reads: 'Caledonian Railway, 6 September; Henry Hughes, platelayer, standing too close to a passing train at the Belmont station, had his foot so severely crushed that death ensued'. 'John Scott, pointsman, in the act of shifting the points at the Clelland Branch, lost his balance and fell under the wheels of a mineral train.' 'Dawson Fieldhouse, waggon inspector, crushed between buffers while uncoupling waggons.'

No mention was made of long hours inducing that inattention, or of poor design or maintenance making such accidents more likely. An *ex-gratia* payment from the railway and something from the provident fund if the deceased had been a member, was the best that the widow could expect. If the man survived and did not recover full health, he might be offered a less demanding post as a gatekeeper or cleaner. Once all accidents to employees had to be registered in 1871, there was a vast increase in the length of these reports; in 1875 no less than 4,383 railwaymen were reported as casualties, 765 of them killed. Twenty years later the total was still as high as 4,392, but the number killed had fallen to 433. By 1966 the number of fatalities to staff had fallen to 140 and has maintained a downward trend as loose-coupled goods trains and their shunters, level crossings and steam engines have disappeared.

Right through the nineteenth century the railways expanded their staff, from about 60,000 in 1850 to half a million at the turn of the century. This meant that there were good promotion prospects for the young man who stuck to his work and was willing to accept responsibility. Once in such a position, he would tend to side with the establishment when disciplining newer recruits, possibly forgetting youthful radicalism. A sure way for management to draw the sting of any incipient industrial action is to promote the activists, a frequent ploy which left a discontented work-force leaderless. The alternative was to sack agitators, but this could lead to solidarity strikes and was to be avoided if possible. The grading of the men into more than a hundred groupings on some railways also aided a 'divide and rule approach'. Signalmen were expected to report enginemen who broke the rules, foremen generally came to hear of the misdeeds of their underlings, so that in closed communities it was difficult if not impossible to keep very much secret. If union membership was frowned upon by management, then either it had to be kept secret or the members had to be numerous enough to practise solidarity. This was evident when the Associated Society of Locomotive Steam Enginemen & Firemen (later known as ASLEF) was formed in 1880. Their proposals included a clause on victimisation: 'Any member having been discharged for having taken an active part in any question relating to hours or wages, or the well-being of his fellow-workmen, to receive a lump sum of £100, and fifteen shillings per week whilst seeking re-employment'. The very large amount, a year's average pay, suggested that the process of getting another job would be difficult.

Despite the tensions generated between unions and management at a time when the former were seen as an unauthorised intrusion on man-to-man dealings, the ASLEF emblem of 1880 had the motto, 'Our employers welfare, public safety and our own protection'. By 1913 that had been changed to 'The public safety and our own protection' after several bruising strikes and confrontations with the likes of Ammon Beasley, the hard man who managed the prosperous Taff Vale Railway. The railway derived most of its profits from moving coal from the pits of the Rhondda and the Taff to Cardiff and Penarth. The conveyor-belt flow was interrupted by pit strikes as well as dock and railway stoppages. The raw immigrant community of native Welsh, Irish and West Countrymen were an unruly lot at the best of times, but the methods used to manage them seem almost guaranteed to make things worse: layoffs without pay when times were bad, followed by long hours of overtime when there were ships waiting at the docks, which made family life very difficult. Management tried to reward those who stayed at work during strikes – the loyal workers who would then be boycotted when work resumed. Even more hated and despised were the blacklegs or 'free workers', sometimes discharged from other railways and desperately seeking employment, others who were drifters who would tackle anything for a pint and a pound. For two decades Ammon Beasley pursued the politics of confrontation. Demands for shorter hours and better conditions were resisted, and in 1900 he took the Amalgamated Society of Railway Servants all the way through the courts to the House of Lords to obtain damages against the union for loss of revenue during the dispute. The unions naturally worked to get this decision reversed, but meanwhile the temperature of Taff Vale confrontations increased as the miners and railwaymen worked together to close down both mines and railways during disputes.

A wave of pit strikes hit the Rhondda and Dare valleys in the autumn of 1910. The miners were so determined to stop everything that they attacked the homes of officials doing essential maintenance work at the Powell Duffryn collieries. Miners still at work in other pits were threatened and hustled as they got off their trains after the shift. Then on 2 November a GWR workmen's train was stormed at Tonllwyd Crossing,

Aberaman, and the passengers attacked. The strike spread, despite a warning that those carrying out these acts could be sentenced to three months with hard labour; in the next fortnight, pits were besieged and sixty policemen had to be used to protect officials giving safety cover. This was possible in compact colliery yards, but a complete railway system could not be so protected and the staff had mixed feelings over joining the strike.

By 20 November action had moved southwards to Tonypandy on the Taff Vale. Ammon Beasley reported that shortly after midnight up to 500 strikers appeared outside the signal-box and two leaders entered, demanding that the signalman stop all trains so that they could be examined for blacklegs; if he did not comply they would wreck the cabin. Local stationmasters had to submit to trains being searched by pickets. There was also a threat to pull up rails unless the company stopped carrying blacklegs. Any blacklegs discovered were held 'in custody' until they could be put on to a train back to Cardiff. Mr Beasley thought it 'intolerable that such a state of things should be allowed to continue', but despite well-publicised police intervention, often after the event, the strike continued into the New Year.

Whether or not the railwaymen supported miners' strikes, the effect of short time on their pay packets led to unrest on the railways. Protests and union activity produced dismissals or victimisation on the Taff Vale. Attempts to introduce railway blacklegs were undertaken by the National Free Labour Association, which brought in a gang of men from London and provincial cities, while the ASRS (later the National Union of Railwaymen) succeeded in persuading the majority to return home on arrival in Cardiff. Very few got to work on the Taff Vale and those who did found their engines slipping on greased rails, wagons breaking loose in the dark and engines failing. Some trains were stoned and loyalist workers were manhandled, but the latter incidents were few.

The unionisation of the work-force in the quarter century

140

before World War I was part of a wider movement in which workmen all over the country rebelled against the conditions imposed in the early years of the railways. Slogans such as, 'In unity strength', started to seem real when the likes of Ammon Beasley could be reduced to frustrated impotence by determined workmen. Activists were still a minority, but they could halt most operations on a national scale in the first countrywide strike in 1911. This happened despite the setting up four years previously of Conciliation Boards on which sat both company and union representatives who were to hammer out points of difference. A sample of such an agreement shows how much things had improved since the days of unco-ordinated memorials and wildcat strikes, but many grievances remained at a time when wages were being kept down and prices were going up:

Meeting of Midland & Great Northern Joint Railways
Conciliation Board No. 2.
*King's Lynn, 23 January 1913.*

    a. HOURS – No signalman to work more than 10 hours per day
    b. OVERTIME – Each day to stand by itself, with time and a half thereafter.
    c. GUARANTEED WEEK – To be applied to all men in the employ of the Committee.
    d. SUNDAY DUTY – At time and a half, not less than a full day's pay.
    e. WAGES – Third class signalman        25/- per week
                  South Lynn Junction signalmen  32/- per week.
    f. YARMOUTH AND MELTON CONSTABLE EAST SIGNAL BOXES – Maximum 8 hour day.
    g. Six days annual holiday for all men employed.

The ominous features of the 1911 strike were that action was co-ordinated with miners and steelworkers at a time when what we would now call an arms race was proceeding with Germany, soon to culminate in World War I. The ASRS, ASLEF and other unions all joined the action as did non-union railwaymen. Stiffnecked managers like George Churchward of the GWR could still feel that if enginemen did not like their conditions they could resign, but others like Sir Vincent Raven recognised that the men should be consulted when major changes were being considered. The amalgamation of the ASRS with two smaller unions to form the NUR in 1913 made the consultations simpler. Of the manual staff, only the footplatemen retained a separate union, with its overtones of Victorian craft separation. A year later the start of war nullified many of the gains of the past few years, but only temporarily. Unionism thrived in war conditions, and the men who served came back determined not to submit to the excesses of the pre-war years.

Long hours and deteriorating conditions in wartime were followed by a frantic boom and inflation on a scale unknown before 1919. The promise of an eight-hour day had been conceded during the war, and national terms and wages for enginemen were agreed with the government which still controlled the railways and the companies that owned them. The lack of an agreement for other railwaymen was the cause of the national strike in September 1919. Despite having achieved their own aims, the enginemen came out in support of other grades. The companies tried to run a skeleton service with the help of loyal railwaymen and civilian volunteers. Troops, including naval stokers, were also used by the Lloyd George government in a strike-breaking exercise. Although the strike only lasted for nine days, much bitterness was caused. There were a large number of incidents: loyalist staff were roughed up, missiles were dropped from over bridges, volunteers were stoned and there was some sabotage. When it was over, the returning strikers refused to work with those who had stayed on duty, making it necessary to post some of them out of the district. J. M. Dunn, author of books and articles on railways, went from Willesden to Abergavenny for this reason.

The early 1920s were a period of retrenchment for the railways. After the profitable war years and the boom which followed, they were faced in 1921 with a massive decline in traffic, competition with buses for their local traffic and high wages at a time when their earnings were declining. Amalgamation, staff reductions and a cutback in expenditure were the response of the companies to the losses of that year. The remainder of Britain's traditional industry was in no happier state. The return to the Gold Standard in 1925 overpriced our exports, particularly coal. Imports on the other hand were cheaper, so attempts were made by employers to cut back wages to make the economy more competitive, a recipe for the increasing strife that led to the General Strike of 1926.

Unlike 1919 the miners, railwaymen, other transport workers and many in manufacturing industry came out at the same time. The miners were the backbone of the strike. They stayed out until the autumn, whereas for most others the strike lasted from Tuesday 4 May until 12 May. As before, the companies (now only four in number) tried to run a service with loyal staff and volunteers. Young sprigs of the nobility, students and professionals rushed to don overalls and try their hand at driving, signalling or firing. Their womenfolk ran the catering services and provided comforts for the volunteers. They managed to run a very sketchy train service; passenger trains were more numerous than goods – about one twentieth of the normal service on 4 May, rising to one sixth by the end – but goods trains were far fewer throughout, not surprising given the closure of the mines and heavy industry and the difficulties of assembling and running the trains. A fair amount of damage was caused by the unskilled driving and firing: fireboxes full of fused clinker, firetubes wedged with lumps of coke and hot axleboxes, were but a few of the maladies which had to be repaired afterwards. On the minimal one day's training received by signalmen it was as well that traffic was very light.

Over half a million railwaymen came out altogether, with support of up to 98 per cent in some grades. It was a show of solidarity that rapidly polarised the two sides. In the absence of newspapers, the radio and government news-sheets gave a radically different story from those put out by the unions. Whether or not a better service could have been achieved had the strike continued we shall never know, but even towards the end there was no more than a small trickle of men back to work.

Many were genuinely surprised when the TUC agreed to a return to work, as they thought they were winning, with the railways unable to provide more than a token service. The men were reinstated subject to traffic, although in the case of those involved with coal traffic, this was not until October or even November. The unions were forced to admit that they had been wrong to call the strike and promised not to do so again without negotiations. Any wildcat strikes were not to receive union support and supervisors were not to be encouraged to strike.

This was not an attempted red revolution as feared by some of the ruling classes. The railways and other older industries were cutting down wages and staff numbers at a time when alternative work was not available. The climb-down by the unions was matched by reasonably civilised terms from the employers, who only refused to re-employ those guilty of violence or intimidation. The worst example of this had been perpetrated by Northumbrian miners at Cramlington on the East Coast main line. On 10 May the southbound Flying Scotsman toppled off the track where a group of nine miners had removed a rail. The train was proceeding under caution, the passengers had been kept out of the front coaches that were derailed, so fortunately no one was hurt. Other miners gave evidence against the accused, resulting in three of them receiving eight-year jail sentences.

The next strike of national importance happened nearly thirty years later in 1955 and involved ASLEF men only. It was a strike in which the minority of NUR footplate men continued working. The railways were sinking into a permanent deficit and the differentials of the footplatemen were being eroded. My father complained bitterly about restaurant car staff and station staff receiving as much as he did, a driver with over thirty years of service. There was no doubting the feeling that drivers and firemen were not sharing in the prosperity of post-war Britain. The Guillebaud Report which followed the strike recommended that pay should be based on comparisons of railway jobs with those in outside industry, rather than on the financial condition of the industry, which was worsening rapidly.

During the strike my father did two spells of picket duty outside Neasden shed in pleasant early summer weather. Money was very short at home, worsened by the fact that I was sent home by the army since there was no work to do in the ordnance depot to which I was posted, with no deliveries by rail. One noticeable feature was the ease of travel. In the absence of trains, car owners were willing to give lifts to servicemen and others, coaches ran to capacity and trucks had never been in such demand. The age of the family car for everyman was dawning, but the railwaymen obtained a better deal, the difference being made up from government grants and capital write-offs, which thenceforth became a regular feature in railway accountancy.

Most union activities are not concerned with strikes; they are about welfare and the just treatment of the work-force. In these activities the unions have been increasingly successful. For the last sixty years, apart from wartime, they have had to cope with staff losses from the all-time peak of about 750,000 railwaymen in 1919 who were divided into innumerable grades, each with its own promotion ladder. The economies of the early grouping years, the depression years and the modernisation programme of the late 1950s were but a prelude to the mass closures and redundancies from 1963 onwards. A slowdown in recruitment and early retirement coped with some of the cascade of job losses that occurred, but when whole systems such as the Southern lines west of Exeter and the lines radiating from Brecon closed, hundreds of men in areas of high unemployment lost their jobs. Works in towns such as Caerphilly, Melton Constable, Inverurie, Oswestry and Darlington were shut down when new working methods dispensed with their services in the mid-1960s. The breaking down of the grading system and the de-staffing of stations, closure and grouping of goods depots, all yielded thousands of redundancies. Yet there were very few stoppages in the orderly rundown of lines, sheds and works. Terms better than the legal minimum terms were negotiated by the unions, but these paled into insignificance in comparison with awards made to the more militant dockers and steelmen in a similar plight. Those who remained worked under improving conditions, as warm cab and padded seat replaced draughty footplate for enginemen, old style goods trains and marshalling yards were replaced by trainload sets and maintenance depots became clean, bright, warm places. Yet management continues to find further ways of slimming a staff to a number smaller than that of 120 years ago. It is good for the accounts but very hard on those constantly fearing for their jobs. Such an atmosphere is a natural breeding ground of discontent and occasional flare-ups.

When there were railway companies, the unions were acutely aware of the dangers of pushing management too far in negotiations. The discipline of the balance sheet affected them too. The governments supervising the nationalised industry abandoned the whip of bankruptcy when they started deficit financing in 1955 and compounded the problem with a modernisation programme which was not internally funded. Vigorous industrial action frequently produced the desired results, especially when aimed against the railway's most vulnerable customer, the London commuter. Attempts to implement staff reductions have therefore met with strong resistance, culminating in the 1982 strikes concerned largely with the issues of single-manning and flexible rostering, which spelt greater efficiency to management but more job losses to the men. The feature most evident in these strikes was how little they slowed down, let alone stopped, the national economy. Newspapers and post were delivered with little interruption, there were no food or fuel shortages and city commuters contrived to get to work, albeit often at great inconvenience. Sir Peter Parker detected a new realism in the wake of the industrial action. Traffic had to be won back with a host of special offers and bulk discounts. Later announcements of further job losses have met with the expected huffing and puffing, but no further industrial action, whilst flexible rostering and single-manning commenced.

A further threat of mass redundancy is implicit in the Serpell Report which sketches a number of scenarios for the future size of the railway system, with a minimal network of under 2,000 miles as a profitable base. This has reinforced the idea that railways must prove their superiority in the things they can do best if they are to retain a much larger network. Commuter trains, inter-city traffic, bulk minerals, speedlink-based freight and containers need to be retained and developed to make a viable system.

The wholesale trimming of administrative staff has started with the closure of divisional offices and the attendant transfers or redundancies. Until the recent computer and word-processor revolution, office staff numbers had proved more resilient than those of enginemen, signalmen and other blue-collar staff. Friends working in the Norwich divisional office have found themselves allocated to York, Cambridge or London at little notice and others prematurely retired, yet the trains still run.

Despite capital starvation, the railway still contrives to give a good service at a lower cost and deficit than richer European neighbours. Only French railways are faster, Dutch more frequent. Many of the staff are proud of achievements made against the odds and it might well change the ideas of press critics if they attended reunions of railwaymen past and present to hear that pride breaking through.

Much damage has been done to the railway community by the posturing on the media of some of the more extreme members of union executives. The lengthy antipathy between the craft union ASLEF and the major manual union, the NUR, in latter years, became almost a personality clash in public between the leaders Ray Buckton and Sid Weighell, both footplatemen from the North East. Both had good traditional reasons for their stances, but only a change in leadership in the NUR has stopped the infighting and started to present a common front which will hopefully result in negotiations in the future which are fair to all concerned. The solid work that goes on all the time behind the scenes to phase in new arrangements, to help to obtain the best deal for sick, elderly or errant members of the railway community, or to prevent management folly, deserves a better public face than hitherto.

Union training has been the major education in public affairs received by numerous distinguished local government counsellors and mayors. Swindon, Carlisle, Peterborough and Norwich, to name but a few, have had railwaymen playing a leading part in local politics. Magistrates, JPs and MPs of impeccable working-class origins have also been produced by the same system, leavening in strong railway areas those with what were once more traditional backgrounds for a place in national or local government.

# 10
# Conclusion

Desire to join the railway service in some capacity has for a century and a half been the great sustaining factor in railway recruitment. Regular work and pay – even if the latter was modest – the chance of promotion in a vast organisation and the opportunity to work elsewhere have encouraged millions of lads to join the railway service in those 150 years. There have been periods of difficulty, especially from 1945 onwards when cleaner, lighter jobs at higher pay could be had for the asking, yet even then enough boys were willing to take on the filthy, demanding jobs with long and unsocial hours.

Love of the steam engine and its works had a lot to do with the attractions of the railway until twenty years ago. The description of it by a nineteenth-century author, Sir George Roney, as 'manacled with harness that Vulcan presided at the forging of – smoke-vomiting, steam-emitting, snorting, bubbling inside, growling – hissing too, with an intensity equal to the combined and concentrated hissing of ten thousand offended and irritated cats', gives something of the flavour that has enthralled generations from their novice days to maturity. Yet railway service extended to millions of other workers who saw but little of train operating. Categories such as lamp porter, carriage searcher, chaff cutter, scavenger and hay checker were also part of the railway community in the past and proud of it. The minute gradations and myriad jobs have disappeared under the label of railman, an attempt to denote an all-purpose operative who can turn his hand to most non-specialist jobs if needed. The diesel engine and unstaffed halts with their low labour requirements have replaced the labour-hungry steam engine and the multi-purpose station, but the devotion lingers on amongst a surprisingly high proportion of the staff. In evoking the past, it is not to denigrate the present generation of railwaymen, but to show how today's situation has come about since *Locomotion*, No 1, first took to the rails.

A service that once had some three quarters of a million men working for it inevitably had many types of humanity employed at any one time, not all of them good. Nevertheless, there is a core of characteristics which taken together gave railwaymen a special esteem in the working-class community. If young recruits were to survive in railway service they had to develop regular habits, a willingness to work what we now term unsocial hours, in the past largely without extra pay, carry out the edicts of the Rule Book in a sensible rather than a dogmatic way, stay sober on duty, be prepared to work on until relief came rather than abandon their post, and always have safety uppermost in their minds. A careless fitter's work should be noticed and reported by a meticulous driver. A driver who ignored a speed limit should be reported by an alert signalman. Slack stationwork, delaying a train and probably also subsequent trains, should be entered in the guard's journal, so that everybody knew that his work was being checked and was thereby kept up to the mark. Where speed and human lives are intertwined, mistakes can be fatal, so discipline was and is something that prevents tragedies. It became a way of life rather than a burden once railwaymen became used to the new conditions of work; punishments became less draconian and accidents fewer by the end of the nineteenth century.

The almost automatic reaction to the disciplines of railway life were visible in the railway community in which the author lived. My father only went to the pub in the evening when he would have a sleep between drinking and driving, so two weeks out of three were dry for him. Getting to work, regardless of weather, war or other worries was regarded as a duty almost above all others. The only exceptions to this were the 1926 General Strike and the ASLEF strike of 1955 and a couple of days towards the end of his career after he had been knocked down by a car. The occupational hazard of lumbago, a toothache or other illness never stopped him from going on duty. The regularity of life and the sense of duty must have been good for the family. It provided us with a steady background, a regularity that could be measured with a watch and some status in the community which rubbed off on other members of the family. I was always referred to as 'Railway Dick's boy' by local shopkeepers, which usually seemed to be worth an extra couple of ounces of meat or a pint of milk when rationing dominated life in the 1940s. The worth of the men who kept the goods moving was appreciated in a working community.

Assembly-line workers often say that the only thing that keeps them working is the money. Except in poorly paid rural areas, railwaymen never became even relatively rich as a result of their employment; indeed for the hours worked, many of them have been paid disgracefully low wages in the past. But withal, boredom is a rarely heard word among railwaymen once they are established in the mystique of their calling. Whether checking the track as a platelayer, shunting goods trains pole in hand or firing a local passenger train, there was always variety in the work. Despite the timetables, no one day was exactly like another, the job usually left scope for initiative and most railway jobs gave some independence and responsibility. Even the major railway works were unlike most factories, being divided into dozens of different shops, each with its own local autonomy, friendships and solidarities. Railways have always been sufficiently attractive for fathers to want their sons to follow them into railway service, hopefully at a higher level. Once established, railway service often goes on for generations, the individuals staying for a lifetime of work. Social life is often based on railway social clubs and societies, especially in railway settlements. Not all areas of employment are so lucky with the attitude of their staff.

The railway companies in pre-grouping days pioneered many of the features of employment that are used by others now to retain long-service staff. Large-scale housing for employees, staff savings banks, sports and recreational facilities, welfare services, holidays, cheap travel, pensions and sick funds all had company blessing and often cash aid from the company. They were administered by the men themselves, who often became adept at management and gave many the grounding that they needed to enter local and national politics. Later, when unions became widespread, they in their turn became the training grounds for aspiring representatives of the people. Self-improvement was not just a term dreamed up by Samuel Smiles, himself a railwayman; it was a means of obtaining promotion to better paid posts, with the top as the upper limit in many cases.

Teamwork is a word frequently heard amongst railwaymen. Driver and fireman in steam days were mates who shared tasks and depended on each other. They in turn depended on plate-layers, signalmen and the remainder of the train crew for their own smooth passage. Their engine was only as good as the shed staff that maintained it. Interdependence was accepted as a fact of life; solidarity was its expression through trade-union activities. The grading system tended to pull away from the unity of railwaymen and there was a feeling of superiority and condescension sometimes on the part of passenger crews *vis-à-vis* goods crews, but on vital matters they closed ranks.

Crises bring out all the best traits in the collective character of railwaymen. The superhuman efforts of staff to help the injured and keep other traffic running in the wake of the Harrow and other disasters have been chronicled elsewhere, but it needs stressing that the ability to help is based on long hours of voluntary training with railway units of the St John Ambulance Brigade or the Red Cross. In wartime traffic well beyond anything seen before or since was carried despite severely reduced staffing and poor maintenance, itself caused by the use of railway works as aircraft and munitions factories. Night after night, through blitz and blackout staff got to work and carried on under inconceivably difficult conditions for sixteen or eighteen hours at a stretch if their relief could not get there. The spirit did not lapse in the post-war period.

A vignette of all that was best in the old railways system was to be found as late as 1952 in an isolated branch line in Suffolk, the former Mid-Suffolk Light Railway. This meandering line from Haughley Junction to the village of Laxfield was set in deepest rural England. It had but two mixed trains a day and the operation was almost entirely divorced from the remainder of the system except for the exchange of goods wagons at Haughley and the dependence on Ipswich engine shed for heavy maintenance and repairs for the single engine in steam. Much of the pre-war atmosphere had been preserved, together with staff qualities that were in retreat elsewhere. It was a microcosm of rural operation which even three decades ago had just about vanished elsewhere.

The guard's van of the goods train was hard up against the buffers at Haughley; several assorted wagons were followed by an incongruous pair of suburban coaches, before reaching the engine heading this motley assortment, a very elderly J15 0-6-0 No 65447. Above the hiss of the steam, the panting of the Westinghouse pump was the loudest noise to be heard in the stillness of the Suffolk countryside after the departure of the Bury train. A blazered, bespectacled lad a few years older than myself was also watching the proceedings. He turned out to be a Cambridge undergraduate playing truant for a day who knew the crew and verified the rumour that one need not travel in the carriages provided. The railwaymen were friendly beyond my wildest hopes, so that my nervous request to travel with the guard met with immediate acceptance: 'Course yer can, lads', as if that were the normal and sociable way to travel in those parts. The Haughley station staff raised no objections, there were no other passengers, so my nervousness evaporated.

'Soo yer whan ter see whaat a guard does?' We followed him down the platform as he visually checked the chain links between the trucks and the brakes to see that they were not on. He must have been noting the tonnage mentally, as he had a total to give the driver at the end of the inspection, as well as writing it in the guard's journal later. Further checks were made to see that the brake pipe at the end of the empty coaches was properly blocked off and that the screw coupling with the leading unbraked wagon was as tight as possible to make the ride as smooth as possible.

'Got some passengers this trip?' asked Driver Skinner. 'It's usually oonly school kids to Stowmarket in the morning, back in the afternoon. Got the day off?' We assured him that we were legally on holiday, then returned to the guard's van, where we were joined by the travelling shunter. A wave of the green flag from the front platform of the van, a shout of 'Hang on tight!', then, after a few seconds of chain rattling together with frantic puffing from the front as the J15 accelerated furiously, the slack was taken up and we suddenly shot forward at 20mph from standstill. The necessity for a frantic start was the steep 1 in 43 bank out of Haughley station yard.

Once the bank was breasted, we settled down to a steady, clanking 20mph, viewing the countryside from the rear platform of the guard's van. The shunter pointed out the sights, the magnificent Suffolk Punch ploughing near Aspall was appraised by both guard and shunter with the eyes of countrymen: 'Take a good look at 'en, 'bor, yer whan't see 'un too much longer with tractors coming on the farms'. Comments on the winter wheat greening the fields, seed drills on the brown expanses of mid-Suffolk all entered my urbanised consciousness and awoke memories of a rural childhood in Cornwall.

Little grey corrugated-iron station buildings on low platforms sported nameboards with fancy cast-iron lettering, made in a local foundry. The staff, where there were any, comprised porter cum gateman cum signalman cum everything else, in a single person. A toot from the engine heralded our arrival. It was a signal to the guard to screw down the handbrake in the van, while the metallic banging of buffers ahead of the van foretold of an instant shock stop. When it came, it was always stomach-turning, so what it was like at the end of a long goods train, I could scarcely bear to imagine.

The shunter hopped down to appraise his duties. The wagons of the train were marshalled in order of dropping, apart from the

Laxfield wagons which were coupled next to the carriages. Aspall, Kenton and Horham required shunting that day. The van and the wagons for further stations were pinned down, while the wagons to be dropped, together with Laxfield's wagons and coaches were uncoupled, pulled ahead to beyond the points, where the chain link was uncoupled. A push from the engine after the points were switched and the wagons rolled into their siding. The points were rapidly switched back again as the remainder of the train was reunited, the shunter running up to the point of impact, coupling up almost on the run. Then, pole crooked under his arm, he hauled himself up the steps of the guard's van before another violent start heralded the next stage of the journey.

By the time the train reached Laxfield, I felt greatly banged about, but much wiser about the job of a train crew. The guard wrote up his journal, omitting to mention his additional passengers and then directed us into the village, while the engine shunted its wagons into the sidings before crossing over the road at the end of the station, disappearing behind the trees to get water at Laxfield Mill. Down the road, the great tower of Laxfield church overshadowed the *Royal Oak*, our lunch-time venue, where sandwiches could be eaten with rough Aspall cider, sitting on wooden benches behind deal tables. The subsequent mock-antique gentrification that it has undergone has not improved it.

On returning to the station, we were gratified to find that the carriages had been cleaned, windows sparkling, and No 65447 was standing tender-first at the head of the carriages and wagons. Our Cambridge friend had heard that footplate rides were not unknown, so as a railwayman's son, I was propelled forward to request a ride. Explaining that my father was a brother footplateman and that we had ridden in the brake van without causing trouble, we soon found the request accepted by driver Skinner and the burly young fireman Law, who said that we could come as far as Kenton with them, where water was to be taken again. The crew were proud of having the most immaculate footplate on British Railways, or so they claimed. It was an easy claim to believe. Driver Skinner had painted the interior of the cab in cream paint in his own time. The brasswork could have done duty as a shaving mirror, while the steelwork was scoured bright. A wire brush was used at frequent intervals to remove soot, coal dust and oil from the footplate and running plate, splashers or anywhere else that steam engine muck might be deposited. This was 'one man, one engine', as in Victorian days. It was a pity that the paintwork was unlined black.

Working tender-first for over two hours would be chilly, but the prospect of a footplate ride made it worthwhile. 'You hold on to the bar over the tender', was the sound advice given us by fireman Law. The rigid six-wheeled tender soon showed us the reason for the advice. Every joint and curve in the track was picked out to give us another jolt, followed by a further shock as the same feature was picked out by the driving wheels a second or two later. The drop-plate between tender and cab was constantly moving to and fro, side to side, plus an occasional buck. The best stance was on the tender side of the drop-plate, feet apart and hanging on for dear life. Fortunately, the firebox had a low appetite, so our fireman had little need to delve with his shovel between our legs while on the move. He stoked up at stations and seemed quietly amused by our efforts to maintain balance between stations. Shunting *en route* was to pick up wagons in the sidings. This time the engine ran forward with the train, minus only the guard's van, coupled on to the new wagons, then back to couple up the brake van before proceeding onwards to Kenton.

Kenton Junction was the proud possessor of the only intermediate signal, which gave a rather ambiguous message to enter the station. Water was taken from the little dammed pond, while a grassy siding to the south indicated the route of the proposed line to Debenham and reason for the 'Junction' on the station title.

The last part of the journey in carriages with barred windows was an anti-climax, but probably easier for the train crew. A fast trip back to London behind one of Bill Harvey's immaculate Britannias was worlds away from pastoral Suffolk.

The railways now employ only a quarter of the numbers that they did at the turn of the century, but they continue to attract a dedicated staff as the early winter of 1979 demonstrated yet again. Hours before dawn the crews of commuter trains reached their frozen depots, and whenever possible the trains ran. Snow-clearing parties had cleared the worst snow drifts on East Anglian lines long before road traffic had started to get through, and although delays were inevitable, nobody was abandoned.

The railway ethos also attracts those who have made their careers outside the railways but still feel drawn to the disciplined activity of running trains. All over the country, on preserved railways from Aviemore to South Devon, Ffestiniog to Sheringham, every weekend and holidays as well, bank clerks, teachers, solicitors, postmen, schoolboys and railwaymen active and retired, to name but a few, freely give their time to scrape rust from a ghost rescued from Barry scrapyard, collect fares, man a signal-box or undertake any one of a huge and essential range of jobs.

# *Appendix*

## NUMBERS OF RAILWAYMEN

| Date | Number | |
|------|--------|---|
| 1849 | 56,000 | Immediately after the Railway Mania |
| 1859 | 116,000 | Railway Mania lines operating, secondary lines being built |
| 1875 | 260,000 | Dense railway network established |
| 1909 | 610,000 | Huge intensification of passenger and industrial traffic |
| 1919 | 750,000 | Post-war boom, shorter hours, prior to economies |
| 1949 | 635,000 | Post-war boom before widespread car ownership |
| 1968 | 318,000 | Five years after the Beeching Report |
| 1982 | 184,000 | Further economies almost continuous |

# Bibliography and Acknowledgements

The main body of this book comes from the personal reminiscences of railwaymen past and present, all of whom seemed greatly to enjoy their careers, despite many rough moments. Even those who left the railways before retirement look back on a past way of life with nostalgia tinged with regret. To my late father, his former shedmaster Bill Harvey, Robert Whatley, Reg Gamble, Ted Cook, Ken Saunders and Norman Sanders as well as to fellow members of the M&GN Circle and others I am greatly indebted.

Of the photographers, Dr Ian C. Allen has recorded it over a long period and his photographs of the Mid-Suffolk Light Railway are without rival. Lens of Sutton, in the person of John L. Smith have produced numerous relevant photographs from many periods, while the National Railway Museum, Leicester Record Office, BR and Locomotive & General Railway Photographs have all been of service. In addition I must thank private persons for their photographic contributions, duly acknowledged.

Libraries and archives have been most helpful in permitting me to see their collections so that I could obtain further background and material. The universities of Leicester, London and East Anglia, the Norfolk and City of Westminster libraries, the Public Record Office, National Museum of Wales and my local branch libraries have all in their various ways contributed to the framework of this book.

The most useful books have been those written by railwaymen themselves at the time. Michael Reynold's *Engine Driving Life* (1880) has yet to be bettered. On the management side, Joseph Tatlow's *Fifty Years of Railway Life* (1920) is far less known than George Neele's contemporary work, but is more readable. In the present century, Alfred Williams' *Life in a Railway Factory* (1915) is a classic of industrial history, while Norman Crump's *By Rail to Victory* (1947) is probably the best of the war histories of the railways and gave further insight into my father's work in the East End during World War II. P. W. Kingsford's *Victorian Railwaymen* gives the facts and figures as well as much detailed background to life on the railways in the nineteenth century. Among trade-union publications, Norman McKillop's *The Lighted Flame* (1950) goes a long way to explain why the engineman loves his job despite the hours and the problems, while Philip Bagwell's magisterial *The Railwaymen* does a very detailed *tour de force* for the NUR.

Numerous journals have been consulted, among them the *Railway Magazine*, *Trains Illustrated*, *Railway World*, *Transport History* and the magazines of the various pre- and post-grouping railways are outstanding for their view on everyday railway life, while journals devoted to particular railways in current circulation add a nostalgic dimension to the last fifty years.

I would also like to thank my wife very much for ferrying endless cups of coffee, brought to my typewriter in the summer house in all weathers; to relatives, friends and students who have listened to parts of the text and made useful suggestions. No book is the sole work of its author. To all those who have helped writing this book wittingly or unwittingly, thank you.

# Index

Marlborough Road station, 37
Marriott, William, 23, 55, 59, 61
Marx, Karl, 19
Marylebone station, 7, 35, 114
Meldon, 118
Melton Constable, 50, 55–61,
134, 145
Metropolitan Railway, 70
Midland & Great Northern Joint
Railway, 24, 29, 30, 32, 50,
53–61, 105, 141
Midland Railway, 17, 21
Midland Great Western Railway
21, 94
Midland & South Western Junc-
tion Railway, 67
Mid-Suffolk Light Railway, 153
*et seq*
Moorgate, 97
Moorsom, Captain, 15
Morrow, Robert, 64
Mundesley, 24
Mutual Improvement Classes, 42

NUR, 140–8
National Free Labour Association,
140
Neasden, 70, 72
Nigeria, 100
North Eastern Railway, 99
North Walsham, 30, 53, 66
North York Moors Railway, 89
Norwich, 102, 132, 147
Nuneaton, 118

Old Oak Common, 74, 75, 101,
131, 132
Oswestry, 145
Oxford, 21

Paddington, 22
Paisley accident, 124

Parker, Leslie, 97
Parker, Sir Peter, 146
Parkes, Charles, 92
Peterborough, 41
Pirrie, Lord, 92
Powell Duffryn collieries, 139
Pressed Steel Co, 63

Queens Park Rangers, 70

ROD, 107
Raven, Sir Vincent, 141
Read, Robert, 54, 55
Red Cross, 152
Rhondda, 139
Robinson, M., 95
Rogers, G., 11
Rolls Royce, 63
Roney, Sir George, 149

St John Ambulance, 152
St Neots, 81
Sandy, 81
Saunders, Ken, 80–9
Severn Tunnel Junction, 31, 133
Shap, 118
Shildon, 47
Simmons, Ernest, 21, 22
Smiles, Samuel, 152
Soham, 116
Somerset & Dorset Railway, 54
Southern Railway, 109
Starlight Specials, 73
Stephenson, George, 10, 18
Stephenson, James, 64
Stockton & Darlington Railway,
9, 47, 64, 136
Stratford, 40, 41, 50, 133
Stratford-upon-Avon & Midland
Junction Railway, 41
Sullivan, Daniel, 20
Swindon, 44–6, 49, 62, 68, 78